An Easter Anthology

An Easter Anthology

Scripture readings, reflections and prayers for
Holy Week and Easter

Compiled by

CANON ARTHUR HOWELLS

With a foreword by Rowan Williams

HODDER &
STOUGHTON

To Margaret and our sons, John and David, in gratitude for all the love we share.

Contents

Foreword

If there is one theme that comes through consistently in this wonderful collection of resources for the Easter season, it is that Easter is far more than a single event, the rising of Jesus of Nazareth from death. Easter uncovers something that is always real at the heart of the created world; it opens the way to a new historical era in which human beings are set free to be more deeply themselves than ever; it shows us how the remembrance of Jesus' life and appalling death may become liberating news for all human beings.

If what is alive in Jesus is nothing less than the whole life of God, then in one way the events of Easter Day are no surprise: test the life of God to the very limit, in violence and rejection, torment and loneliness, and it remains alive. If it didn't, creation itself would fall apart. And from another perspective, it is the supreme moment of surprising newness: who could have imagined that life could be like *this*? that not even the most desolate and terrible moments of our experience would be left without companionship, witness, compassion and hope?

Arthur Howells does a superb job of weaving together these insights about death and resurrection, past, present and future, in a rich sequence of readings and prayers, reminding us why the early Church thought of the whole period between Easter Day and Whitsunday was a time of continuing celebration, exploring the life of a new creation. He invites us in to this exploration with depth and simplicity, in a way that believers of all ages and backgrounds can relate to.

This book will be a great inspiration for anyone who wants to grasp more fully why Christians say that they are 'an Easter people', and how the Easter story shapes our prayer, our advocacy and our action in a world where the darkness of Good Friday is so visible in so many lives. As we pray in the Easter Vigil service, 'May the light of Christ, rising in glory, banish all darkness from our hearts and minds.'

Rowan Williams
Cardiff 2022

Introduction

In the latter half of the fourth century Egeria, a Spanish nun, was given permission by her community to spend several Easters in Jerusalem where she was to observe the ways in which Christians were keeping Holy Week and Easter. Fortunately, Egeria kept a detailed diary in which she recorded all the events that took place during the days from Palm Sunday through Maundy Thursday, Good Friday and Easter. Her record demonstrates that the services and accompanying ceremonies were all linked together like one long play commemorating the various acts and scenes associated with the passion and resurrection of Jesus. Today, in her liturgies, the Christian Church has inherited many of these approaches to the Paschal drama that were displayed in fourth-century Jerusalem. While Christian communities of our own day derive much spiritual benefit from the liturgical services held during this solemn period in the Church's year, it has also been found helpful to accompany these outward observances with some special acts of devotion. People are encouraged to spend time throughout Lent, for example, enriching their daily prayer with readings and devotional commentaries on the events of Jesus' life and their meaning for today. They make the journey to Easter in company with Jesus using the reflections of spiritual authors alongside the scriptures to draw closer to him. Such are the contents of this anthology: a scripture passage, a reading and a prayer. You will notice that this book concentrates on the Easter season – from Easter Day to Pentecost, sometimes called 'The Great Fifty Days' to distinguish it from the forty days of Lent. However, we can't have Easter without Holy Week when we observe the events leading up to our Lord's passion and his death on the cross. In this volume we see these events through the lens of many gifted spiritual writers who bring us new insights in our commemoration of the last days of Jesus' life and his subsequent resurrection.

After the birth of Jesus and the worship of the shepherds we are told by St Luke that 'they made known what had been told them about this child; and all who heard it were amazed at what the shepherds told them. But Mary treasured all these words and *pondered* them in her heart'. 'Pondering' means to make space to think, to consider and to pray. This involves taking time out, being still and silent and using the scripture passage and the reflection that follows as points of contemplation. We ask ourselves: 'What is God saying to me through these words?' and then 'What do I want to say to him?' using the prayer that follows, perhaps as a springboard for our own prayer. As we follow the events of our Lord's passion and resurrection day by day we can associate ourselves more closely with the characters involved – their doubts, fears, loves, hopes and longings.

There are many ways of using this book. The reflections can be a source of prayer for us or it may be helpful to meet with a friend or neighbour spending time pondering over the reflections. Alternatively, you may like to use the book for a group meeting once a week after you have completed each week's readings, sharing what you have been learning.

In a group you may like to ask each other:

1. Which of the readings has meant most to you?
2. What have you found difficult to understand?

3. Is there some way in which you would like to respond to what you have discussed?

One of our writers, Anthony Bloom, says: 'The joy of the resurrection is something which we must learn to experience, but we can experience it only if we first learn the tragedy of the cross.' I pray that this may be true of us as we make this journey together.

Arthur Howells
Advent 2022

An Easter Anthology

Suddenly

As I had always known
he would come unannounced,
remarkable merely for the absence
of clamour. So truth must appear
to the thinker; so, at a stage
of the experiment, the answer
must quietly emerge. I looked
at him, not with the eye
only, but with the whole
of my being, overflowing with
him as a chalice would
with the sea. Yet was he
no more there than before,
his area occupied
by the unhaloed presences.
You could put your hand
in him without consciousness
of his wounds. The gamblers
at the foot of the unnoticed
cross went on with
their dicing; yet the invisible
garment for which they played
was no longer at stake, but worn
by him in this risen existence.

R. S. Thomas

HOLY WEEK

PALM SUNDAY

He who comes in the name of the Lord

*A*s they approached Jerusalem and came to Bethphage and Bethany at the Mount of Olives, Jesus sent two of his disciples, saying to them, 'Go to the village ahead of you, and just as you enter it, you will find a colt tied there, which no one has ever ridden. Untie it and bring it here. If anyone asks you, "Why are you doing this?" say, "The Lord needs it and will send it back here shortly."'

They went and found a colt outside in the street, tied at a doorway. As they untied it, some people standing there asked, 'What are you doing, untying that colt?' They answered as Jesus had told them to, and the people let them go. When they brought the colt to Jesus and threw their cloaks over it, he sat on it. Many people spread their cloaks on the road, while others spread branches they had cut in the fields. Those who went ahead and those who followed shouted,

'Hosanna!'

'Blessed is he who comes in the name of the Lord!'

'Blessed is the coming kingdom of our father David!'

'Hosanna in the highest heaven!'

Jesus entered Jerusalem and went into the temple courts. He looked around at everything, but since it was already late, he went out to Bethany with the Twelve.

Mark 11:1–11

3

It was the time of festival ... Jerusalem was overwhelmed with pilgrims, and with merchants trying to provide them with provisions and services. Why would you pick Jesus out from all the other pilgrims? He is not the only one with a colt (meaning here an ass or donkey). Donkeys were the white vans of the day. There were lots of them.

There was, of course, the strange way that he had acquired it. Did he have second sight, or was it pre-arranged? Or is he commandeering it in the name of God, like a king could commandeer goods and services in a time of war? So – was he God's king coming in power to recapture the city and the world and bring about the kingdom of God? But if he was and is, what sort of power is he coming with? Mark does not mention it, but as we look on might we hear the echo of Zechariah 9:9 where the king coming on a donkey rather than a war horse means that he is coming in peace? Is the power of Jesus not that of authority and might, but the power of self-giving love?

As people went up to the temple, the streets were steep and became slippery. People might well have put cloaks and branches down to help provide a grip. Or were they making an impromptu red carpet in homage to him?

As they went up they would also be singing the festival songs or psalms. These were a bit like an opera or a musical, in that they told a story and different voices sang different parts. You can find two of them in what we know as Psalm 24 and Psalm 118 ...

So was Jesus a pilgrim coming in amongst all the other pilgrims? Or a king coming into his kingdom? Or a representative of God coming into God's house? Or some sort of a mixture of all those? Whatever the answer, people would have seen things in various ways at the time. Some things would only become clear as the disciples looked back with hindsight after the crucifixion and resurrection.

'Who do you say that I am?' said Jesus in and through it all. He still says it to us now. What do we make of him, in our lives and our world?

From Holy Week Worship for the Methodist Church, 2021

L ord Jesus Christ,
  you humbled yourself in taking the form of a servant,
and in obedience died on the cross for our salvation:
grant us the faith to know you and love you,
that we may be found beside you
on the way of the cross,
which is the path of glory;
give us the mind to follow you
and to proclaim you as Lord and King,
to the glory of God the Father. Amen.

Adapted from *Common Worship*

MONDAY IN HOLY WEEK

The temple

When Jesus entered the temple courts, he began to drive out those who were selling. 'It is written,' he said to them, '"My house will be a house of prayer"; but you have made it "a den of robbers".'

Every day he was teaching at the temple. But the chief priests, the teachers of the law and the leaders among the people were trying to kill him. Yet they could not find any way to do it, because all the people hung on his words.

Luke 19:45–8

Jesus was increasingly coming to understand that, staggering as it may sound, he was not only to inaugurate God's kingly rule (or Kingdom), he was not only to cleanse the Temple in order that it should be a worthy throne for the King, but that Temple was to be a flesh and blood one – a living seat of mercy! He himself was to incarnate the Temple, to be the 'temple-in-person' ...

His ultimate obedience would be through oblation and death. The Temple was, above all, the place of sacrifice. And somehow he came to see himself as both the Temple and the sacrificial lamb – Temple, Priest and Victim all in one!

The original enticement in the wilderness had been to purify the Temple by jumping from a pinnacle and landing miraculously unharmed. His mission, as Jesus came to perceive it, was to be the exact opposite. It was not simply to purge the existing Temple but to become a new one. Not to do his purifying work without any personal harm – but rather *through* pain and the way of destruction. No longer would it be a place where year by year thousands upon thousands of innocent lambs were slaughtered – but one perfect Lamb would become the guilt-offering and provide a full, perfect and sufficient sacrifice for the sins of many (cf. The Book of Common Prayer, Prayer of Consecration). It would be the sacrifice to end all animal sacrifices. It would be a new and *living* way to God; it would be a self-willed offering of total love and obedience 'costing not less than everything', an offering with the potential to bring all people to the Father.

From *The Hidden Face of Jesus*, Sister Margaret Magdalen CSMV

L *ord Jesus,*
   you entered the temple,
overturned the tables of the moneychangers,
throwing out the dovesellers with the words of the prophet –
My house shall be called a house of prayer:
make your home in the temple of our hearts
and dwell there for ever. Amen.

TUESDAY IN HOLY WEEK

The better part

*A*s Jesus and his disciples were on their way, he came to a village where a woman named Martha opened her home to him. She had a sister called Mary, who sat at the Lord's feet listening to what he said. But Martha was distracted by all the preparations that had to be made. She came to him and asked, 'Lord, don't you care that my sister has left me to do the work by myself? Tell her to help me!'

'Martha, Martha,' the Lord answered, 'you are worried and upset about many things, but few things are needed – or indeed only one. Mary has chosen what is better, and it will not be taken away from her.'

Luke 10:38–42

Our reflection today takes the form of a meditation in which we spend time slowly pondering on the story, picturing the scene and entering into the meeting Jesus has with Martha and Mary. Listen to what Jesus has to say to them and what he has to say to you.

You find yourself by a simple dwelling on the edge of a village. You find yourself with Jesus and some of his disciples being invited by the woman Martha into her house. What sort of a room is it? . . . And as Jesus sits and begins to speak you notice others settling down to listen and Martha's sister Mary sits at Jesus's feet . . . Where are you in the room? . . . Are you standing or do you decide to sit? . . . What does Mary look like, what is she wearing? What does Jesus begin to talk about?

Martha has been busy preparing and serving food. How aware have you been of her busyness in the background? . . . Perhaps she moves the dishes in such a way as to make some extra noise to draw attention to all that she is about. Maybe she bustles in and out rather ostentatiously.

Finally, when Jesus pauses, Martha interrupts, 'Lord, do you not care that my sister is leaving me to do all the serving by myself? Please tell her to help me.' How does Mary react to those words? . . . Jesus says, 'Martha, Martha, you worry and fret about so many things, and yet few are needed, indeed only one. It is Mary who has chosen the better part; it is not to be taken from her.'

Let the story now gently unfold. Let Martha sit down and rest awhile, listening to Jesus who carried on speaking . . . or does she go back about her business? Does anyone else do anything? . . . Perhaps someone goes to help her? . . . What do you decide to do? . . .

What does Jesus say now? ... Soon some will be leaving. Does Jesus come with you or does he stay on? ... Maybe there is an exchange of words at the door, maybe there is a gesture or acknowledgement of your presence, by Mary, by Martha or by Jesus? Anyway, finally you find yourself standing once again beside the house. You go into the village. Take a moment to notice how you are ... and then bring this to a close.

From *On Retreat – A Lenten Journey*, Andrew Walker

WEDNESDAY IN HOLY WEEK

The seamless robe

*J*ust then a woman who had been subject to bleeding for twelve
years came up behind him and touched the edge of his cloak. She
said to herself, 'If I only touch his cloak, I will be healed.'

*Jesus turned and saw her. 'Take heart, daughter,' he said, 'your
faith has healed you.' And the woman was healed at that moment.*

Matthew 9:20–2

*Near the cross of Jesus stood his mother, his mother's sister, Mary the
wife of Clopas, and Mary Magdalene. When Jesus saw his mother
there, and the disciple whom he loved standing near by, he said to her,
'Woman, here is your son,' and to the disciple, 'Here is your mother.'
From that time on, this disciple took her into his home.*

*Later, knowing that everything had now been finished, and so that
Scripture would be fulfilled, Jesus said, 'I am thirsty.' A jar of wine
vinegar was there, so they soaked a sponge in it, put the sponge on a
stalk of the hyssop plant, and lifted it to Jesus' lips. When he had
received the drink, Jesus said, 'It is finished.' With that, he bowed his
head and gave up his spirit.*

John 19:25–30

He carried a seamless robe. It was a thing of delicate beauty and of great craftsmanship, robust and at the same time light, woven in one piece from top to bottom, like the robe a high priest would wear as he went about his duties.

Like everything else, it would be taken from him.

Freshly made, it billowed from the loom as it was released, completed. The freshness and the newness of it made you want to bury yourself in its folds. Or else just put it on. The fingers that spun it, the hands that made it, held together in satisfaction of a job well done. For things crafted have a lasting value: but one that is easily squandered ... Laundered and hung out to dry it drifted in the breeze.

But there was no breeze that day. The air seemed to hang in the sky like a great leaden weight: like the yellowing clouds of smog that stain our own cities. Somewhere a fire was crackling. Dogs barked. Children cried out in fear and stared in bemused amazement.

His sweat and blood stained the cloth. It clung to him, and where it had been lashed, the fibres of the material stuck to the congealing wounds.

Around the hem, where the stitching was plain to see, the material was starting to fray. Something was unravelling, becoming undone.

And on another day, in another crowd, one would reach out to touch his hem. Not to admire its beauty, or measure the quality of the cloth, but to come as close as one could to touching the man, to feel his pulse and know the energy of his life. And even in a crowd, with hundreds jostling around him, clamouring for attention, he would cry out, 'Who touched me?', as if this were something obvious. But he could tell. He could be pressed in on every side and still discern each touch. You see, there are no crowds for him, only people, each one a thing of beauty, each one delicately and unrepeatably distinct. He sees each face, knows each name, feels each touch and knows its meaning.

What do you want me to do for you?

From *The Things He Carried*, Stephen Cottrell

*Y*ou felt her touch and knew her need.
 The healing power within you was yours to share
and she received it, for her prayer was heard.
So, Lord, as you know each of us by name and
we are valued in your sight,
shed your healing love on us.
Fill us with the energy and power of your Spirit
and make us whole
that we may serve you to the end,
our Master and our Friend.

MAUNDY THURSDAY

True humility

*I*t was just before the Passover Festival. Jesus knew that the hour
had come for him to leave this world and go to the Father. Having
loved his own who were in the world, he loved them to the end.

The evening meal was in progress, and the devil had already
prompted Judas, the son of Simon Iscariot, to betray Jesus. Jesus knew
that the Father had put all things under his power, and`that he had
come from God and was returning to God; so he got up from the
meal, took off his outer clothing, and wrapped a towel round his
waist. After that, he poured water into a basin and began to wash his
disciples' feet, drying them with the towel that was wrapped round
him.

John 13:1–5

The foot-washing constitutes an invitation not only to learn a lesson but also to follow an example. It is recorded and re-enacted not only to provoke our admiration but our emulation. It is meant to touch our imaginations and to set us wondering: 'Could I do that?', 'Should I do that?' and '*Shall* I do that?' Jesus' example is meant to challenge our aspirations; to suggest to us that we could learn how to do this ... This involves not seeking to meet the needs of the poor on our own terms but *envisioning* a radically different future. They are the sort of questions that embolden people to face reality and enter into the vulnerability of risk-taking. This is the point of the foot-washing. It is not that the feet needed a wash, but that the disciples needed a new set of attitudes. Discipleship might seem to involve meeting the needs of others but at a more radical level it is about doing the things that cause us to be changed in heart and mind. Focusing on the needs of others is a tried and tested way out of excessive self-concern and interest. But it only works, so to speak, if it leads us to discover that the other has more to offer us than we them. This is the flip-side of the famous quote that if you want to change the world you must start with yourself. The reality is that if you seriously go about trying to change the world for the better, you yourself will be more profoundly transformed in the process than 'the world'. I wonder whether it is too much to call that transformation 'being humbled'. Certainly those who engage with passion and empathy in the cause of justice often speak of being humbled when they come up for air. We should cheer when they do so, and seek the path of our own humbling.

From *Barefoot Disciple*, Stephen Cherry

L ord Jesus,
　as you humbly took a basin and towel
and washed the feet of your friends,
cleanse us
that following your example
we, too, may be servants
who wash the feet of those in need
in tenderness and love. Amen.

GOOD FRIDAY

The victory of the cross

*P*raise be to the God and Father of our Lord Jesus Christ! In his
great mercy he has given us new birth into a living hope through
the resurrection of Jesus Christ from the dead, and into an inheritance
that can never perish, spoil or fade. This inheritance is kept in heaven
for you, who through faith are shielded by God's power until the
coming of the salvation that is ready to be revealed in the last time. In
all this you greatly rejoice, though now for a little while you may have
had to suffer grief in all kinds of trials. These have come so that the
proven genuineness of your faith – of greater worth than gold, which
perishes even though refined by fire – may result in praise, glory and
honour when Jesus Christ is revealed. Though you have not seen
him, you love him; and even though you do not see him now, you
believe in him and are filled with an inexpressible and glorious joy,
for you are receiving the end result of your faith, the salvation of your
souls.

1 Peter 1:3–9

'It is accomplished!' Jesus has achieved all he came to do. And yet in a sense it is not yet finished. For when we speak of the cross we don't simply mean the suffering of Jesus. We use the word as a kind of shorthand by which we mean God's love declaring itself through this completely offered man, through his whole life, death and resurrection and what follows. For what then follows is the eager and loving response of men and women ever since. The fulfilment of Christ's life and death comes through people identifying themselves with him, living in and by his Spirit, offering themselves to God in trust and becoming open to his life. And this must go on to the end of time.

'It is accomplished!' We mustn't forget that St John is writing all this not just in the light of Easter but as one who for much of his life has lived and worshipped in the Church born of the resurrection, and there is in this penultimate word a real sense of victory – a foretaste of Easter. The seven words from the cross between them speak both of desolation and of glory: St Mark and St Matthew focus on the agony but St John tells the story with a title above and beneath and wrapped all about it, and that title is the word 'glory'. The way Jesus meets his death, with trust and with forgiveness on his lips, is this final act of self-giving love, and that is the very glory of being God himself.

So Good Friday is a victory. Easter confirms it but it doesn't make it one, for it is a victory already. What Easter does is to bring its power into human lives in any age for those who live in the Spirit of the risen Christ.

'It is accomplished!' When they nailed Jesus to the cross they placed above his head a placard to make people smirk – Jesus of Nazareth, the King of the Jews. And they said, 'Let him reign from there!'

Let him reign from there! The existence of your church and my church and every church in Christendom, and the witness of the whole company of saints and martyrs, known and unknown, and the witness of countless Christians who in times of suffering and anguish have continued to put their trust in God, prove that he does.

From *Dust that Dreams of Glory*, Michael Mayne

O Lord Christ, Lamb of God, Lord of Lords,
    call us, who are called to be saints,
along the way of your Cross:
draw us, who would draw nearer our King,
to the foot of your Cross:
cleanse us, who are not worthy to approach,
with the pardon of your Cross:
instruct us, the ignorant and blind,
in the school of your Cross:
arm us, for the battles of holiness,
by the might of your Cross:
bring us, in the fellowship of your sufferings,
to the victory of your Cross:
and seal us in the kingdom of your glory
among the servants of your Cross,
O crucified Lord;
who with the Father and the Holy Spirit
lives and reigns, one God
almighty, eternal, world without end.

Adapted from *A Procession of Passion Prayers*, Eric Milner-White

EASTER EVE (HOLY SATURDAY)

Waiting in the shadows

*L*ater, *Joseph of Arimathea asked Pilate for the body of Jesus. Now Joseph was a disciple of Jesus, but secretly because he feared the Jewish leaders. With Pilate's permission, he came and took the body away. He was accompanied by Nicodemus, the man who earlier had visited Jesus at night. Nicodemus brought a mixture of myrrh and aloes, about thirty-five kilograms. Taking Jesus' body, the two of them wrapped it, with the spices, in strips of linen. This was in accordance with Jewish burial customs. At the place where Jesus was crucified, there was a garden, and in the garden a new tomb, in which no one had ever been laid. Because it was the Jewish day of Preparation and since the tomb was near by, they laid Jesus there.*

John 19:38–42

It's a relief to acknowledge the disappearance of God on Holy Saturday and the uncertainty of the outcome. That's not to say that we remove ourselves from the hope of the resurrection, but we admit that hope doesn't prevent the bleakness of God's apparent absence from descending even upon those with the strongest faith. C. S. Lewis wrote in *A Grief Observed* that when you are happy and feel no particular need of God, he seems to be there and welcoming you with open arms:

> But go to Him when your need is desperate, when all other help is vain, and what do you find? A door slammed in your face, and a sound of bolting and double bolting on the inside. After that, silence. You may as well turn away. The longer you wait, the more emphatic the silence will become.

As their hopes for a new future evaporated overnight, the disciples faced instead a great chasm of grief as God vanished from sight with no promise that he would ever return. The magnitude of grief they faced on Holy Saturday was because they believed that Jesus was gone for ever.

It's a common experience, when people are first bereaved, that they do not feel the impact of the loss. Their loved one still feels present to them; the death hasn't yet had time to sink in. There is a great deal to be done just to organise a funeral, and in those first few days they can be swept along, carried by the warmth and sympathy and kind words of friends. It's often a few days after the funeral that the real bleakness begins. Friends and relatives return to their normal routine, and the bereaved person has to go back to theirs – except that for them, nothing will ever be normal again. That's when the absence of the loved one starts to become real, as a strange and unwelcome future opens up like a blank white page.

This is what Holy Saturday is: the absence of God, and the uncertainty and emptiness of being uprooted. Easter faith was born in the darkness and, like the disciples, sometimes we just have to wait in the shadows until eventually a glimmer of light appears on the horizon.

From *Giving It Up*, Maggi Dawn

*L*ord, help us to accept
that though there are times
when you seem to be absent —
those dark and lonely days —
you are always with us
though hidden from our sight.
Fill us with hope as we wait and pray;
for you have defeated death
and live and reign for ever.

EASTER

FIRST WEEK OF EASTER

EASTER DAY

A time of hope

*F*or what I received I passed on to you as of first importance: that Christ died for our sins according to the Scriptures, that he was buried, that he was raised on the third day according to the Scriptures, and that he appeared to Cephas, and then to the Twelve. After that, he appeared to more than five hundred of the brothers and sisters at the same time, most of whom are still living, though some have fallen asleep . . . Whether, then, it is I or they, this is what we preach, and this is what you believed.

1 Corinthians 15:3–6, 11

E aster season is a time of hope. There still is fear, there still is a painful awareness of sinfulness, but there is also light breaking through. Something new is happening, something that goes beyond the changing moods of life. We can be joyful or sad, optimistic or pessimistic, tranquil or angry, but the solid stream of God's presence moves deeper than the small waves of our minds and hearts. Easter brings the awareness that God is present even when his presence is not directly noticed. Easter brings the good news that, although things seem to get worse in the world, the Evil One has already been overcome. Easter allows us to affirm that although God seems very distant and although we remain preoccupied with many little things, our Lord walks with us on the road and keeps explaining the Scriptures to us. Thus there are many rays of hope casting their light on our way through life.

From *Show Me the Way*, Henri Nouwen

*L*ift me up, Risen Lord,
    from the darkness within
    to the light of your presence.

Lift me up, Risen Lord,
    from despair and depression
    to hope and love.

Lift me up, Risen Lord,
    from the hidden places within
    to the peace of your presence.

Lift me up, Risen Lord,
    from the fears of today
    to the challenges of tomorrow.

Reach down to me
    that I may know that nothing
    can separate me from your love.

EASTER MONDAY

No chance encounters

*N*ow *that same day two of them were going to a village called
Emmaus, about seven miles from Jerusalem. They were talking
with each other about everything that had happened. As they talked
and discussed these things with each other, Jesus himself came up and
walked along with them; but they were kept from recognising him.*

*He asked them, 'What are you discussing together as you walk
along?'*

*They stood still, their faces downcast. One of them, named
Cleopas, asked him, 'Are you the only one visiting Jerusalem who
does not know the things that have happened there in these days?'*

'What things?' he asked.

*'About Jesus of Nazareth,' they replied. 'He was a prophet,
powerful in word and deed before God and all the people . . .'*

Luke 24:13–19

If he would stick to the impractical white robe and sandals even in winter, I might be able to pick Jesus out in a crowd. I might still mistake him for the homeless person, almost literally a bundle of rags, who sits on the sidewalk by my subway station. I might mistake him for the taciturn surgeon who once saved my life. I might mistake him for one of our parish teenagers who isn't too grown up to give me a spontaneous hug that almost knocks me over. I might mistake him for the total stranger who offers me the gift of a tiny act of random kindness. I might mistake him for the unacceptable person, the blemish on my carefully maintained landscape. The list goes on and on. And on.

If nothing else, the story of this encounter is a powerful reminder of the sheer ordinariness of miracles. All too often we recognise them only in retrospect.

Perhaps it is more accurate to call this walk to Emmaus a *seemingly* chance encounter. As I look back on my decades, I realize more and more that there are really no accidents, no chance encounters. No matter how twisted or straight the road might seem, no matter what unlikely folk might join us for a few feet or a few miles, our walk is not a casual wandering. If we see our lives as the long walk between two thresholds, we know that, while it can be lonely, it can never be solitary. Yes, there are good companions like the unnamed disciple who walked with Cleopas. Yes, there are other encounters – some of them dangerous, some annoying, and many of them unexpected. These are chance encounters with the holy, those seemingly random encounters with Jesus, the inveterate walker.

He just shows up with no appointment and not dressed as we expect. He refuses to look the part as he walks among us.

From *Walking Home*, Margaret Guenther

*L*ord Jesus Christ,
stay with us, too, we pray
in every part of the journey;
when the going is tough and
when the going is smooth,
no matter how full of doubt and fear
we may be.

Through your Holy Spirit
open our eyes.
Help us to see you as our Risen Christ
in all your beauty and in all your loving power.

EASTER TUESDAY

A pattern we can trust

*D*ear friends, since God so loved us, we also ought to love one another. No one has ever seen God; but if we love one another, God lives in us and his love is made complete in us.

This is how we know that we live in him and he in us: he has given us of his Spirit. And we have seen and testify that the Father has sent his Son to be the Saviour of the world. If anyone acknowledges that Jesus is the Son of God, God lives in them and they in God. And so we know and rely on the love God has for us.

God is love. Whoever lives in love lives in God, and God in them.

John 4:11–16

To believe that Jesus was raised from the dead is actually not a leap of faith. *Resurrection and renewal are, in fact, the universal and observable pattern of everything.* We might just as well use non-religious terms like 'springtime,' 'regeneration,' 'healing,' 'forgiveness,' 'life-cycles,' 'darkness,' and 'light.' If incarnation is real, if material creation is inspirited, then resurrection in multitudinous forms is to be fully accepted. Or to paraphrase a statement attributed to Albert Einstein, it is not that one thing is a miracle, but that the whole thing is a miracle!

If divine incarnation has any truth to it, then resurrection is a foregone conclusion, not a one-time anomaly in the body of Jesus, as our Western understanding of the resurrection felt it needed to prove – and then it couldn't.

The Risen Christ is not a one-time miracle but the revelation of a universal pattern that is hard to see in the short run (Romans 5:5; 8:9) by the Spirit dwelling within us.

Simply put, if death is not possible for the Christ, then it is not possible for anything that 'shares in the divine nature' (2 Peter 1:4). God is by definition eternal, and God is Love (1 John 4:16), which is also eternal (1 Corinthians 13:8), and this same Love has been planted in our hearts (Romans 5:5; 8:9) by the Spirit dwelling within us. *Such fully implanted Love cannot help but evolve and prove victorious, and our word for that final victory is 'resurrection.'* Peter states this rather directly: 'By raising Jesus Christ from the dead, we have a sure hope and the promise of an inheritance that can never be spoiled or soiled or fade away. It is being kept for you in the heavens … and will be fully revealed at the end of time' (1 Peter 1:3–5).

My book *The Universal Christ* is about the Eternal Christ, who never dies – and who never dies *in you*! Resurrection is about the whole of creation, it is about history, it is about every human who has ever been conceived, sinned, suffered, and died, every animal that has lived or died a tortured death, every element that has changed from solid, to liquid, to ether, over great expanses of time. It is about you and it is about me. It is about everything. The 'Christ journey' is indeed another name for every thing.

From *The Universal Christ*, Richard Rohr

*L*oving Lord,
  as we give thanks for the miracle of the resurrection
we pray that, as your pilgrim people,
we may know that you have planted Love in our hearts
by the Spirit dwelling within us,
and that we may ever witness to this truth
as we make the Christ journey.

EASTER WEDNESDAY

He is the way

A *s they approached the village to which they were going, Jesus
continued on as if he were going further. But they urged him
strongly, 'Stay with us, for it is nearly evening; the day is almost over.'
So he went in to stay with them.*

*When he was at the table with them, he took bread, gave thanks,
broke it and began to give it to them. Then their eyes were opened and
they recognised him, and he disappeared from their sight. They asked
each other, 'Were not our hearts burning within us while he talked
with us on the road and opened the Scriptures to us?'*

*They got up and returned at once to Jerusalem. There they found
the Eleven and those with them, assembled together and saying, 'It is
true! The Lord has risen and has appeared to Simon.' Then the two
told what had happened on the way, and how Jesus was recognised by
them when he broke the bread.*

Luke 24:28–35

Christ's Passover to the Father is our Passover; Christ's long, dark journey is ours, and ours is his. He is in us and we are in him. In no part of the journey and in no place of failure are we ever alone. It is joyful because of him; there is always beauty along the road, and the certainty of his love. Prayer is our willing communion with a mystery of love far greater than our ideas or hopes or plans or vision, and as we fail bitterly in life and in prayer itself we are gently helped to bypass our limited expectations. Distress and bewilderment, knowing yet not knowing, the burning hearts, the realization afterwards that amid all the unknowing we did know, the closeness of Christ in word and sacrament: all this is an inspired picture of how things are, since Easter, along the road. He is more than a wayfarer with us; he is the Way.

Prayer is a long search, a dark journey; if we think of it as a journey to God we are not altogether wrong, but it is also a journey with God and a journey in God. He is not someone over against us, with whom we have to conduct a conversation or form a relationship. 'In that day', said Jesus, the day which dawned at Easter and will see us into eternal life, 'in that day you will know that I am in my Father, and you in me, and I in you' (John 14:20). There is nothing, 'no-thing', between you and God.

From *Gateway to Hope*, Sister Maria Boulding

L ord, give me faith –
     faith to perceive you,
faith to receive you,
faith to understand you,
faith to know you,
that as I draw near to you
and receive your love
so I may dwell in you
and you in me,
my Risen Lord.

EASTER THURSDAY

Mary at the tomb

*N*ow Mary stood outside the tomb crying. As she wept, she bent over to look into the tomb and saw two angels in white, seated where Jesus' body had been, one at the head and the other at the foot.

They asked her, 'Woman, why are you crying?'

'They have taken my Lord away,' she said, 'and I don't know where they have put him.' At this, she turned round and saw Jesus standing there, but she did not realise that it was Jesus.

He asked her, 'Woman, why are you crying? Who is it you are looking for?'

Thinking he was the gardener, she said, 'Sir, if you have carried him away, tell me where you have put him, and I will get him.'

Jesus said to her, 'Mary.'

She turned towards him and cried out in Aramaic, 'Rabboni!' (which means 'Teacher').

Jesus said, 'Do not hold on to me, for I have not yet ascended to the Father. Go instead to my brothers and tell them, "I am ascending to my Father and your Father, to my God and your God."'

Mary Magdalene went to the disciples with the news: 'I have seen the Lord!' And she told them that he had said these things to her.

John 20:11–18

This stunning invitation comes as Mary acts out one of the oldest dramas in the world. Stand with her as she weeps. Think of someone you know, or have seen on television or in the newspapers, who has cried bitterly this last week. Bring them too, and stand there with Mary. Don't rush it. Tears have their own natural rhythm. Hold them – the people, the tears in your mind as you stand outside the tomb. And then, when the moment is right, stoop down and look into the tomb itself. Be prepared for a surprise.

Where had the angels come from? They hadn't been there a few moments before, when Peter and John had been inside the tomb. Or maybe they had been. Maybe sometimes you can only see angels through tears. Whatever. When people are afraid, angels tend to tell them not to be. When people are in tears, angels ask why. Say it out loud. Whoever you've brought with you to stand here, listen to them say it too. They have taken away ... my home, my husband, my children, my rights, my dignity, my hopes, my life. They have taken away my master. The world's grief, Israel's grief, concentrated in Mary's grief.

Now, as you stand with Mary and ponder her answer and the answers the question would receive today from around the world, turn around and see the strange figure who's standing there. Who is he? What's he doing? Who do you think he is?

From *John for Everyone*, Tom Wright

We bring before you, compassionate Lord,
those who weep today,
those who see you through tears,
those who have lost hope,
those whose pain lies in the empty tomb.
May they see through their tears you, the Risen Lord.
May they hear you calling them by name.
May they know that their absent loved ones
are now in the nearer presence of you,
the One who lives for evermore.

EASTER FRIDAY

Hope reborn

If God himself has taken up residence in your life, you can hardly be thinking more of yourself than him. Anyone, of course, who has not welcomed this invisible but clearly present God, the Spirit of Christ, won't know what we are talking about. But for you who welcome him, in whom he dwells – even though you still experience all the limitations of sin – you yourself experience life on God's terms. It stands to reason, doesn't it, that if the alive and present God who raised Jesus from the dead moves into your life, he'll do the same thing in you as he did in Jesus, bringing you alive to himself? When God lives and breathes in you (and he does, as surely as he did in Jesus), you are delivered from that dead life. With his Spirit living in you, your body will be alive as Christ's.

Romans 8:9–14, *The Message*

After a century of numerical decline in a culture when indifference to the gospel shows signs of turning into hostility towards it, it is not surprising that the people of God should see themselves as a beleaguered and ageing minority whose hopes cannot extend far beyond their own short-term survival, with all the debilitating consequences that entails for the life of the fellowship. The only possibility of escape from such a situation is a repentant turning round away from the survey of discouraging trends around us and to a fresh engagement with the gospel that has the risen Jesus as its centre. When Mary Magdalene looked at the empty tomb where all her hopes were lost, she wept, but when she turned round and, at his word, recognised the risen Jesus, her expectations became boundless and her extinguished hopes were reborn.

In dark moments of the church's life, the risen Jesus calls us to turn round again to his risen presence, which in practice means to open ourselves in prayer to the springs of life at the heart of our gospel until we come into revitalising contact with the great 'But God' of Easter morning. This is the God who, at the moment when things are at their most hopeless, can act decisively to reverse the trend and, at the very moment when all seems lost, can stage a resurrection.

From *Praying with Paul,* Tom Smail

God's presence be in me,
God's love encircle me,
God's power surround me,
God's peace calm me,
God's healing make me whole,
God's presence be in me
now and always.

EASTER SATURDAY

Room for doubt?

*N*ow *Thomas (also known as Didymus), one of the Twelve, was not with the disciples when Jesus came. So the other disciples told him, 'We have seen the Lord!'*

But he said to them, 'Unless I see the nail marks in his hands and put my finger where the nails were, and put my hand into his side, I will not believe.'

A week later his disciples were in the house again, and Thomas was with them. Though the doors were locked, Jesus came and stood among them and said, 'Peace be with you!' Then he said to Thomas, 'Put your finger here; see my hands. Reach out your hand and put it into my side. Stop doubting and believe.'

Thomas said to him, 'My Lord and my God!'

Then Jesus told him, 'Because you have seen me, you have believed; blessed are those who have not seen and yet have believed.'

John 20:24–9

Whatever strength of faith we have – definite or doubting, firm or frail, certain or sceptical – it's OK either way. God loves us unconditionally, however certain we are or however many doubts we have. When it comes down to it, it is not about how convinced any of us are. To be called to follow Christ is not to absorb hand-me-down information or to be conformed into clones who believe exactly the same thing. There's always room for doubt and challenge. In fact, questions and doubts often result in learning and enlightenment.

Having doubts does not make us a heretic; having doubts simply makes us human. The real heresy is claiming to be a follower of Jesus but then not living out his love and compassion towards one another and the planet. Faith is about our attitudes and actions, our hope and vision. It's about delicately holding the joy and challenge of Jesus in a wonderful balance. It's about glimpsing the kingdom in our very earthly, difficult and draining lives. It's about opening our hearts to a God who cannot be contained in a creed or, indeed, in any human words. After all, our God, as we celebrate at Easter, could not be contained in a box – or, indeed, in a tomb. Jesus' call is, therefore, not a call to conformity. Rather it is a call to transform our world through his love.

From *Opening Our Lives*, Trystan Owain Hughes

R isen Christ,
thank you for sharing the journey with me,
for the joy of knowing
that you are always with me
even when I doubt whether the effort is worthwhile.
I greet you with your followers
here and everywhere.

Risen Lord,
your light has broken through
the darkness of the world.
Let it irradiate our hearts
that we may be bringers of peace and hope
and heralds of joy
transforming the world with your love.

Alleluia! Alleluia!

SECOND WEEK OF EASTER

SECOND SUNDAY OF EASTER

'I am the dance, and I still go on'

F or this reason I kneel before the Father, from whom every family in heaven and on earth derives its name. I pray that out of his glorious riches he may strengthen you with power through his Spirit in your inner being, so that Christ may dwell in your hearts through faith. And I pray that you, being rooted and established in love, may have power, together with all the Lord's holy people, to grasp how wide and long and high and deep is the love of Christ, and to know this love that surpasses knowledge – that you may be filled to the measure of all the fullness of God.

Ephesians 3:14–19

God raised Jesus from the dead; but the resurrection of his body was and is, by all accounts, something very different indeed from a mere continuation of his bodily life, as if the two days among the dead were just a hiccup in the story of the physical Jesus. The French have got it extremely wrong in speaking of *le Christ ressuscité*, as if he had merely come back to life again, as if the resurrection of Christ were in the same class as the raising of Jairus' daughter. This is the start of something completely different, a wholly new form of life and being: 'Even if we used to know Christ according to the flesh,' says St Paul, 'yet now we no longer know him (so)' (2 Cor. 5:16).

That was certainly the experience of the disciples in the gospel story. It is strange that, in the resurrection narratives, they again and again fail to recognise the risen Christ: in the garden, on the road to Emmaus, in the Upper Room, by the lakeside. Although at first he does have some sort of appearance, it clearly isn't physical in the ordinary sense: he appears and disappears, he gets through locked doors, he can't be held down. And in the fourth Gospel, where in a sense we are dealing throughout with the risen Christ, he is presented not just in human and physical terms, but as transcending physical laws – changing water to wine, walking on the sea, multiplying the loaves, raising the dead – and in a whole series of powerful and bewildering images: as bread, wine, light, truth, life. I AM he declares again and again, echoing God's word to Moses: he is eternally present, not constrained by time and space ... '*I am the Lord of the dance, and I still go on*'. During his earthly life, he was leader of the dance; now he actually *is* the dance.

From *Bread of the World*, John Hadley

66

They cut me down and I leapt up high;
I am the life that'll never, never die;
I'll live in you if you'll live in me –
I am the Lord of the Dance, said he.

Dance, then, wherever you may be;
I am the Lord of the Dance, said he,
And I'll lead you all, wherever you may be,
And I'll lead you all in the Dance, said he.

Sydney Carter (1915–2004) © 1963 Stainer & Bell Ltd

MONDAY

A sign of peace

*O*n the evening of that first day of the week, when the disciples were together, with the doors locked for fear of the Jewish leaders, Jesus came and stood among them and said, 'Peace be with you!' After he said this, he showed them his hands and side. The disciples were overjoyed when they saw the Lord.

Again Jesus said, 'Peace be with you! As the Father has sent me, I am sending you.'

John 20:19–21

What does it mean to offer Christ's peace to each other? For many people exchanging the peace is rather embarrassing. We might offer a peck on the cheek to members of our family or friends, but strangers are more likely to receive a distant nod or a handshake ...

When we offer each other a sign of peace we are not so much making peace as accepting the gift of Christ's peace. When Mahatma Gandhi died, he had just one picture in his room, of the risen Christ, and under it a quotation: 'He is our peace' (Ephesians 2:14). This is a peace which our squabbling cannot destroy. In the beginning God said, 'Let there be light' and there was light. At the beginning of the new creation, God's Word said, 'Peace be with you', and it is. In ancient burial grounds in Rome, the inscriptions record that people died '*in pace*', in peace. This simply means that they died as members of the Church that is Christ's peace, even though they fought just as much as we do. To be a member of the Church is to share Christ's peace, however perturbed we may feel ...

At the Last Supper Jesus sat at table with the disciples in real but imperfect communion. He then embraced all the ways in which our communication is faulty, subverted or betrayed. In hope, he took into his hands their fear, betrayal, incomprehension, saying 'This is my body, given for you'. To encounter the risen Christ, then, is to be present to the one in whom lies, cowardice, misunderstanding and even death are defeated. He is thus really present, more present than we are to each other, more bodily. The Eucharist is the sacrament of the 'real presence' of Jesus. On Easter Sunday he overcame all the absences – the distances, silences, misunderstandings, disloyalties by which we are separate from one another and from God. He is truly the embodied Word of God which breaks through every barrier. That is what it means for him to say, 'Peace be with you'. For him to be risen is, then, not just to be alive once more: it is to be the place of peace in which we meet.

From *Why Go to Church?*, Timothy Radcliffe

Peace be with you,
Peace within you,
Peace to fill you,
Peace to calm you,
Peace to free you,
Peace to surround you,
Peace to share
with friend and stranger.
The Peace of the Lord
be with you always!

TUESDAY

Dying we live

Since, then, you have been raised with Christ, set your hearts on things above, where Christ is, seated at the right hand of God. Set your minds on things above, not on earthly things. For you died, and your life is now hidden with Christ in God. When Christ, who is your life, appears, then you also will appear with him in glory.

Colossians 3:1–4

The joy of the Resurrection is something which we must learn to experience, but we can experience it only if we first learn the tragedy of the Cross. To rise again we must die. Die to our hampering selfishness, die to our fears, die to everything which makes the world so narrow, so cold, so poor, so cruel. Die so that our souls may live, may rejoice, may discover the spring of life. If we do this then the Resurrection of Christ will have come down to us also. But without the death on the Cross there is no Resurrection, the Resurrection which is joy, the joy of life recovered, the joy of the life that no-one can take away from us anymore! The joy of a life which is superabundant, which, like a stream runs down the hills, carrying with it heaven itself reflected in its sparkling waters. The Resurrection of Christ is reality in history as his death on the Cross is real, and it is because it belongs to history that we believe in it. It is not only with our hearts but with the totality of our experience that we know the risen Christ. We can know him day after day as the Apostles knew him. Not the Christ of the flesh, not Christ as he was seen in bewilderment by people who surrounded him in the days of his earthly life, but the everliving Christ. The Christ of the spirit of whom St Paul speaks, the risen Christ who belongs to time and eternity because he died once upon the Cross but lives forever. The Resurrection of Christ is the one, the only event which belongs both to the past and to the present. To the past because it did happen, on a given day, in a given place, at a given moment, because it was seen and known as an event in time, in the life of those who had known him. But it belongs also to every day because Christ, once risen, is ever alive, and each of us can know him personally, and unless we know him personally we have not yet learnt what it means to be a Christian.

From *Meditations on a Theme*, Anthony Bloom

L ord God,
  help us to be honest with you
and with ourselves
as we look for answers to those questions
which arise within us.
Give us the faith to accept that as you,
our Risen Lord, were present to Mary, John, Peter
and the other disciples,
so you are alongside us now, calling us by name,
within us and around us.

WEDNESDAY

The glory of God's love

F or what we preach is not ourselves, but Jesus Christ as Lord, and ourselves as your servants for Jesus' sake. For God, who said, 'Let light shine out of darkness,' made his light shine in our hearts to give us the light of the knowledge of God's glory displayed in the face of Christ.

But we have this treasure in jars of clay to show that this all-surpassing power is from God and not from us. We are hard pressed on every side, but not crushed; perplexed, but not in despair; persecuted, but not abandoned; struck down, but not destroyed. We always carry around in our body the death of Jesus, so that the life of Jesus may also be revealed in our body. For we who are alive are always being given over to death for Jesus' sake, so that his life may also be revealed in our mortal body. So then, death is at work in us, but life is at work in you.

It is written: 'I believed; therefore I have spoken.' Since we have that same spirit of faith, we also believe and therefore speak, because we know that the one who raised the Lord Jesus from the dead will also raise us with Jesus and present us with you to himself. All this is for your benefit, so that the grace that is reaching more and more people may cause thanksgiving to overflow to the glory of God.

Therefore we do not lose heart. Though outwardly we are wasting away, yet inwardly we are being renewed day by day. For our light and momentary troubles are achieving for us an eternal glory that far outweighs them all. So we fix our eyes not on what is seen, but on what is unseen, since what is seen is temporary, but what is unseen is eternal.

2 Corinthians 4:5–6, 13–18

Now that I am retired I go early almost every morning to a holy space at the far end of Salisbury Cathedral called the Trinity Chapel. The east window, made in Chartres by Gabriel Loire, is dedicated to prisoners of conscience. Its three central lancets present Jesus as a prisoner of conscience whose stand for truth to the point of crucifixion has inspired and strengthened those men and women all over the world who challenge the lie in whatever form, and face torture and death in their own stand for truth and justice. At first, in the bleak winter months, no light penetrates the window and it appears as a darkly monochrome jigsaw of indecipherable glass. But gradually, as Morning Prayer begins, the dawn light seeps through the glass and the first colour to appear is glass of the palest blue: the glass in the shape of a long widening triangle stemming from the head of the cross on which the body of Jesus hangs, and this extended blue triangle lights up the faces of the prisoners, some holding crosses, some held in symbolic chains, in the lower part of the window. The next colour to appear is a blood-red crimson. It surrounds the hanging body of Jesus. It finds echoes in some of the prisoners' clothing. Finally, as the Eucharist gets under way, a shower of gold appears in the very apex of the window above the crucified, gold suggesting the glory of the self-giving love of God as that is seen in the suffering and death of Jesus; gold that also speaks of resurrection.

Blue and crimson and gold. I do not know of any modern work of art which most successfully connects our human story, the story (at its most testing) of those men and women who even now endure what Dietrich Bonhoeffer called 'the suffering of God in the life of the world', to that most powerful story of all, the story that can both change us as the pattern of our own journey continues to unfold.

From *Pray, Love, Remember*, Michael Mayne

A lmighty Father,
whose Son was revealed in majesty
before he suffered death upon the cross:
give us faith to perceive his glory,
that glory revealed in a life of self-giving,
that we may be strengthened to suffer with him
in costly acts of generous love,
and be changed into his likeness from glory to glory;
who is alive and reigns with you and the Holy Spirit,
one God, now and for ever.

THURSDAY

The new age has begun!

I have revealed you to those whom you gave me out of the world. They were yours; you gave them to me and they have obeyed your word. Now they know that everything you have given me comes from you. For I gave them the words you gave me and they accepted them. They knew with certainty that I came from you, and they believed that you sent me. I pray for them. I am not praying for the world, but for those you have given me, for they are yours. All I have is yours, and all you have is mine. And glory has come to me through them. I will remain in the world no longer, but they are still in the world, and I am coming to you. Holy Father, protect them by the power of your name, the name you gave me, so that they may be one as we are one. While I was with them, I protected them and kept them safe by that name you gave me. None has been lost except the one doomed to destruction so that Scripture would be fulfilled.

I am coming to you now, but I say these things while I am still in the world, so that they may have the full measure of my joy within them. I have given them your word and the world has hated them, for they are not of the world any more than I am of the world. My prayer is not that you take them out of the world but that you protect them from the evil one. They are not of the world, even as I am not of it. Sanctify them by the truth; your word is truth. As you sent me into the world, I have sent them into the world. For them I sanctify myself, that they too may be truly sanctified.

John 17:6–19

What really happened that Sunday evening when the disciples met together? Did they begin to tell each other stories? Did Mary Magdalene relate once more how she had seen the Lord, and what he had said to her? Did John open his heart and mind to the others, and tell them how in the tomb that morning he had seen things in a new light and been grasped by a new truth? Did Peter burst in with the news 'he has appeared to me also'? ... We are told as much in St Luke's gospel, and also that the two disciples from Emmaus came knocking urgently on the locked door of the house, their hearts on fire with the story of how a stranger had walked with them and sat down to supper in their house, and that when he took bread, blessed it, broke it and gave it to them, 'their eyes were opened and they knew him'. Did the whole gathering of disciples then break bread together, as Jesus had commanded them to do three days earlier 'in remembrance of me'? As they gave the bread to each other, were their eyes opened to see the real presence of the crucified Jesus standing amongst them in the eternal depth of that present moment? Did he show them his glory, and give them to each other? Did the new commandment begin to spring out of their hearts and minds – 'love one another as I have loved you' – for 'I AM the resurrection' had really come and was standing in their midst? ...

He gives them to each other as he has given Mary to John and John to Mary, and he commissions his disciples not only to carry his peace in their own hearts and in their lives together, but also to let it transform the world. *Then Jesus said to them again, 'Peace be with you. As the Father has sent me, so I send you.'*

From *Water into Wine*, Stephen Verney

*L*ord of Life,
  fill me with your Spirit,
  in disappointment and distress,
  in fear and doubt,
  in pain and sorrow.

Lord of Life,
  fill me with your Spirit,
  in sickness and in health,
  when all seems lost
  and I feel forgotten.

Lord of Life,
  fill me with your Spirit,
  when I am angry and hurt,
  when I feel unloved and unwanted
  and at war within myself.

Lord of Life,
  give me your peace,
  that peace which passes all understanding.

Lord of Life,
  fill me with your Spirit
  and, above all,
  help me to be a peace maker
  and a peace sharer.

FRIDAY

The power of the Risen Christ

' *F*or through the law I died to the law so that I might live for God. I have been crucified with Christ and I no longer live, but Christ lives in me. The life I now live in the body, I live by faith in the Son of God, who loved me and gave himself for me. I do not set aside the grace of God, for if righteousness could be gained through the law, Christ died for nothing!'

Galatians 2:19–21

The Resurrection has power to transform our lives. The more we accept its truth, its reality, the greater will be the change in our attitudes towards God and in our view of the world in which we live.

Sin and death did not triumph over Jesus Christ; indeed they could not, for the man Jesus Christ was also God. When one day we shall see God as he truly is, we shall understand the riches and fullness of life itself with all its wonder and all its beauty. We shall realise too that perfection and the origin of all love is in him. These things lie beyond us now; they are beyond our understanding. But we can see enough to know that life and love in Jesus Christ could not *possibly* be extinguished, could not be defeated. With him, they would, so to speak, rise again and become then his gift to us.

He wants to give us his love. He wants to give us his life. He will do so if we wish to receive them from him. This is what St Paul meant when he wrote: 'Now the life you have is hidden with Christ in God' (Col. 3.3). New life has been given to us. We receive it first at Baptism. That life made St Paul say on another occasion: 'I live now, not I, but Christ lives in me' (Gal. 2.20). Bold words but full of significance. We must not think of Christ rising from the dead and then leaving us to cope as best we can, to live as he taught us how. No, he remains with us, present always, unseen by the eye and beyond the touch of the hand. Through our faith we come to realise more and more his presence within us and around us. Jesus Christ lives.

From *To be a Pilgrim*, Cardinal Basil Hume

The Lord is risen! And we are risen with him.
The Lord is risen! And life eternal is ours.
The Lord is risen! And death has lost its sting.
The Lord is risen! And the way to heaven is open.
The Lord is risen! He is risen indeed.
Alleluia!

SATURDAY

Unlock the doors!

*I*n that day this song will be sung in the land of Judah:

> *We have a strong city;*
> *God makes salvation*
> *its walls and ramparts.*
> *Open the gates*
> *that the righteous nation may enter,*
> *the nation that keeps faith.*
> *You will keep in perfect peace*
> *those whose minds are steadfast,*
> *because they trust in you.*
> *Trust in the* LORD *for ever,*
> *for the* LORD, *the* LORD *himself, is the Rock eternal.*

Isaiah 26:1–4

The following combines both a reflection and a prayer.

*T*he *funeral party was over.*
   The crisis past.
You were dead.
Your disciples, Lord, met together behind locked doors.
That room is the place to which a person goes to cope with hopes
that are unfulfilled.
That room is the room of disappointments.
And there they met.

But there too they were met, encountered by you, Lord.
You came alive in a group of the disappointed.
You brought peace and joy to their hearts.
You transformed them from disillusion to excitement.
You transformed them from closed group behind locked doors
to people prepared to live and speak openly as your followers.
No angels here, no pomp and pageantry.
Just an ordinary situation, ordinary people meeting together in sorrow.

Lord, come alive within my experience,
within my sorrows and disappointments and doubts,
within the ordinary moments of my life.
Come alive as the peace and joy and assurance
that is stronger than the locked doors within,
with which we try to shut out life.
Come alive as the peace and joy and assurance that
nothing in life or death can kill.

From *A Kind of Praying*, Rex Chapman

THIRD WEEK OF EASTER

THIRD SUNDAY OF EASTER

From fear to faith

*W*hither shall I go from thy spirit: or whither shall I flee from
    thy presence?
If I climb into heaven thou art there:
if I make my bed in the grave thou art there also.
If I fly on the wings of the morning:
or alight in the uttermost parts of the west,
even there shall thy hand lead me:
and thy right hand shall hold me.
If I say 'Surely the darkness shall cover me:
and my day be turned into night,
the darkness is no darkness with thee, but the night is as clear as
    the day:
the darkness and the light are both alike.

Psalm 139:6–11, *The Revised Psalter*

Mary Magdalen's story is not discouragingly triumphalistic. We can identify with her fragility, her devastation in the face of disappointment. Hopefully, if we too have stood in the place of tears, weeping over a loss which seems tragic and final, we can, through reflecting on her journey to the empty tomb, enter into a more vital experience of the Risen Lord and hear him saying again to us (almost as though he were just at our elbow): 'Fear not! I have called you by name. You are mine.' And we spring up from the depths of our own 'Rabboni'. We, too, feel the need to cling to him – not in a neurotic paralysis of fear, but because hand-in-hand with him we shall grow in that perfect love which both transfigures us and frees us to find our true selves.

When the grey days come and the 'dark nights' of the soul, when our spirits flag and we mourn the loss of former spiritual consolations, this woman with her impetuosity and vigour encourages us to search, to look into the emptiness, to face it squarely, to recognise that once more the Lord has eluded us as we looked for him in the expected place or way. But she points us to a radical new experience of resurrection where the grave of our hopes becomes the gateway to a new dimension of relationship with the Risen Jesus. We dry our tears, turn from our tombs and discover for ourselves the everlasting Easter of the Heart. It is the way of Mary Magdalen – the joyful journey she made from pain to passion, lust to love, fear to faith, doubt to dancing.

From *Transformed by Love*, Sister Margaret Magdalen

*L*ord,
you created and fashioned me,
you know me and searched me out.
You abide with me through light and dark:
help me to know your risen presence in this life
that I may be transformed into your likeness
and discover the everlasting Easter of the Heart.

MONDAY

Welcome one another

*F*or everything that was written in the past was written to teach us, so that through the endurance taught in the Scriptures and the encouragement they provide we might have hope.

May the God who gives endurance and encouragement give you the same attitude of mind toward each other that Christ Jesus had, so that with one mind and one voice you may glorify the God and Father of our Lord Jesus Christ.

Romans 15:4–6

It always seems strange to me that Jesus was not readily identifiable after his resurrection. Perhaps there is a sign in this that Jesus is always coming to us 'in another form' (see Luke 24:33–5). We recall how St Francis of Assisi in the days leading up to his conversion dismounted from his horse to embrace a leper, and in him saw the face of Christ. Or how St Benedict taught his brothers that they were to receive one another and the guests to the monastery as Christ himself among them. In the well-known words of Albert Schweitzer, 'Christ comes to us as one unknown without a name, just as of old by the lakeside he came to those men who knew him not.' Yet for this truth we need not go beyond our Lord's own words: 'I was hungry and you fed me; naked and you clothed me; sick and you visited me ... Inasmuch as you did it to one of these my little ones you did it to me' (Matthew 25:35, 36, 40).

We, too, are to find Christ in one another ... But let it be said that if anyone finds Christ in us, it is the Christ in them which has seen the Christ in us, and so the Christ in them is available for us to recognise and feed on if we have not already done so. In so far as we become aware that everyone is a bearer of Christ to us, to that degree we shall bring Christ to them. Not that we shall be conscious of it, for it seems to be almost a law of the spiritual life that we give out most when we are least aware that we are giving out anything at all.

'Receive one another', says St Paul, 'as Christ Jesus received you.' And how does he receive us? – graciously, patiently and with great compassion. Knowing how much we ourselves stand in need of the patience and compassion of Christ mediated through others, so too we are mediators of Christ to them. Thus we shall be Christ-bearers to one another, each finding in the other the agent of our deliverance.

From *Thirsting for God*, Robert Llewelyn

*A*ll through this day, dear Lord,
may we see you in each other,
recognise you,
reverence you,
receive you,
and converse with you
as you shared yourself
with two friends on the Emmaus Road.

As you broke the bread
and broke the Word,
so may we know
and love you
and serve you,
our Risen Lord.

TUESDAY

'I will be with you, I am with you'

'*Do not fear, for I have redeemed you;*
I have summoned you by name; you are mine.
When you pass through the waters,
I will be with you;
and when you pass through the rivers,
they will not sweep over you.
When you walk through the fire,
you will not be burned;
the flames will not set you ablaze.
For I am the LORD *your God,*
the Holy One of Israel, your Saviour;
I give Egypt for your ransom,
Cush and Seba in your stead.
Since you are precious and honoured in my sight,
and because I love you,
I will give people in exchange for you,
nations in exchange for your life.
Do not be afraid, for I am with you;
I will bring your children from the east
and gather you from the west.'

Isaiah 43:1–5

What if our hearts are closed and fear prevents us from opening the doors? The good news is that Christ, now risen, can come through closed doors to deliver us. Closed doors are not a barrier to him: *Although the doors were shut, Jesus came and stood among them and said, 'Peace be with you!'*

This takes us into the real meaning of resurrection. Resurrection is not about going through wooden doors or walls: this would be magic. Resurrection is this new capacity that Jesus has acquired to reach us wherever we might be lost or imprisoned. *Resurrexi et adhuc tecum sum*, 'Risen, I am with you always', runs a wonderful Latin Gregorian antiphon for Easter – a sentence that exquisitely captures the essence of the resurrection. The most insistent promise and assurance God utters in the Old Testament is this *I will be with you, I am with you.* Jesus is the fulfilment of this promise. His name is *Emmanuel, that is God with us*, but only with the resurrection is this promise realized. Only then can Jesus be everywhere at all times in the power of his Spirit so that neither distance, nor darkness, nor even our wish to flee away from him, can escape the reach of his love and presence anymore.

Yes, the risen Christ can reach down to the deepest corners where we are hiding, prisoners of our loneliness, our fears, our anxieties, our despair, our depressions, our cynicism, our shame, and there he shows us his hands and his side. This is an important gesture. It is Jesus' way of saying to us: 'I know what you are suffering because I shared it. I know your sadness because I felt it, I know your feeling of having been abandoned by God because I screamed it, I know your loneliness because I was betrayed by all my friends. But thanks to me all this suffering has become a source of life, light, peace and joy, and it reopens the doors, it abolishes the walls, it restores the relationship with the Father.'

From *Say it to God*, Luigi Gioia

R isen Lord,
come and reach down to us.
Awaken us to your presence,
open the doors of our hearts,
show us the path of life.
Help us to know that you are with us
as you were with the disciples
behind the closed doors
of the Upper Room
and like them,
we have nothing to fear.

WEDNESDAY

The saving presence

'Sir,' the woman said, 'I can see that you are a prophet. Our ancestors worshipped on this mountain, but you Jews claim that the place where we must worship is in Jerusalem.'

'Woman,' Jesus replied, 'believe me, a time is coming when you will worship the Father neither on this mountain nor in Jerusalem. You Samaritans worship what you do not know; we worship what we do know, for salvation is from the Jews. Yet a time is coming and has now come when the true worshippers will worship the Father in the Spirit and in truth, for they are the kind of worshippers the Father seeks. God is spirit, and his worshippers must worship in the Spirit and in truth.'

The woman said, 'I know that Messiah' (called Christ) 'is coming. When he comes, he will explain everything to us.'

Then Jesus declared, 'I, the one speaking to you – I am he.'

John 4:19–26

Our doors are closed because we are afraid of the Father, just like the prodigal son who travelled to a far country, and because we are afraid of each other. Yet Jesus comes, wherever we are, he reaches us, we discover him among us, in us, and we hear him as he repeats to us his reassuring 'Peace to you'. 'Do not let your heart be troubled, do not be afraid, it is I' (cf. Jn 14.1).

Our life of prayer begins when we finally experience this presence of the risen Lord, which brings peace, joy, freedom, hope – when we finally hear him saying in the depths of our hearts: 'Peace be to you'. This is why resurrection and prayer are inseparable; the resurrection is not a reality that we see, but a presence that we discover – not outside us, but within, in our inmost being. And thus prayer becomes a matter of learning to wait in faith and in hope for the risen Lord to enter into our locked selves, just as he entered the locked room where the apostles waited in discouragement and fear.

So the hour is coming, and is now here, when the true worshippers will worship the Father in spirit and in truth (Jn 4:23). It has come because Christ is risen, because we are no longer alone, locked in ourselves, because our hearts have become the place where we can at last find a saving presence, a presence that gives us peace. Prayer is now the space where we welcome the fruits of the resurrection.

From *Say it to God*, Luigi Gioia

*R*isen Christ,
sometimes our hearts are troubled
and we are full of fear;
we become discouraged
and fail to trust you.

We ask you to help us to remember
that we are never alone
and that our hearts can become
the place of peace where you dwell,
your temple,
and live with us for ever.

THURSDAY

Risen with Christ

*S*ince, *then, you have been raised with Christ, set your hearts on things above, where Christ is, seated at the right hand of God. Set your minds on things above, not on earthly things. For you died, and your life is now hidden with Christ in God. When Christ, who is your life, appears, then you also will appear with him in glory. Therefore, as God's chosen people, holy and dearly loved, clothe yourselves with compassion, kindness, humility, gentleness and patience.*

Colossians 3:1–4, 12

The two disciples as they walk and talk on the Emmaus Road:

We recall Jesus' words from [Maundy] Thursday night about his body and blood. We remember what happened on [Good] Friday when his body and blood were separated from one another on the cross. That's what crucifixion was, we realise: the slow, excruciating, public separation of body and blood. So, we wonder, could it be that in the holy meal, when we remember Jesus, we are making space for his body and blood to be reunited and reconstituted in us? Could our remembering him actually re-member and resurrect him in our hearts, our bodies, our lives? Could his body and blood be reunited in us, so that we become his new embodiment? Is that why we saw him and then didn't see him – because the place he most wants to be seen is in our bodies, among us, in us?

It's dark when we reach Jerusalem. Between this day's sunrise and today's sunset, our world has been changed for ever. Everything is new. From now on, whenever we break the bread and drink the wine, we will know that we are not alone. The risen Christ is with us, among us, and within us – just as he was today, even though we didn't recognise him. Resurrection has begun. We are part of something rare, something precious, something utterly revolutionary.

It feels like an uprising. An uprising of hope, not hate. An uprising armed with love, not weapons. An uprising that shouts a joyful promise of life and peace, not angry threats of hostility and death. It's an uprising of outstretched hands, not clenched fists. It's the 'one day' we have always dreamed of, emerging in the present, rising up among us and within us. It's so different from what we expected – so much better.

That is what it means to be alive, truly alive. This is what it means to be en route, walking the road to a new and better day. Let's tell the others: The Lord is risen! *He is risen indeed! The* Lord is risen! *He is risen indeed!* The Lord is risen! *He is risen indeed!*

From *We Make the Road by Walking*, Brian D. McLaren

Loving Lord,
you are the resurrection and the life.
Raise us, we pray,
from death to all that is sinful
to share in your risen life
and to live as your people
sustained by the bread and wine,
your body and blood.
We pray that we may live in you
and that you will live in us.

FRIDAY

A feast of hope

For this reason, ever since I heard about your faith in the Lord Jesus and your love for all God's people, I have not stopped giving thanks for you, remembering you in my prayers. I keep asking that the God of our Lord Jesus Christ, the glorious Father, may give you the Spirit of wisdom and revelation, so that you may know him better. I pray that the eyes of your heart may be enlightened in order that you may know the hope to which he has called you, the riches of his glorious inheritance in his holy people, and his incomparably great power for us who believe. That power is the same as the mighty strength he exerted when he raised Christ from the dead and seated him at his right hand in the heavenly realms, far above all rule and authority, power and dominion, and every name that is invoked, not only in the present age but also in the one to come. And God placed all things under his feet and appointed him to be head over everything for the church, which is his body, the fullness of him who fills everything in every way.

Ephesians 1:15–23

The message about Easter is not primarily a message about Jesus' body, although we have been trained to limit it to this one-time 'miracle'. We've been educated to expect a lone, risen Jesus saying, 'I rose from the dead; look at me!' I'm afraid that's why many people, even Christians, don't really seem to get excited about Easter. If the message somehow doesn't include us, humans don't tend to be that interested in theology. Let me share what I think the real message is: *Every message about Jesus is a message about all of us*, about humanity. Sadly, the Western church that most of us were raised in emphasized the individual resurrection of Jesus. It was a miracle that we could neither prove nor experience, but that we just dared to boldly believe.

But there's a great secret, at least for Western Christians, hidden in the other half of the universal church. In the Eastern Orthodox Church – in places like Syria, Turkey, Greece, and Egypt – Easter is not usually painted with a solitary Jesus rising from the dead. He's always surrounded by crowds of people – both haloed and unhaloed. In fact, in traditional icons, he's pulling people out of Hades. Hades is not the same as hell, although we put the two words together, and so we grew up reciting in the creed that 'Jesus descended into hell.'

Instead, Hades is simply the place of the dead. There's no punishment or judgement involved. It's just where a soul waits for God. But we neglected that interpretation. So the Eastern Church was probably much closer to the truth that the resurrection is a message about humanity. It's a message about history. It's a corporate message, and it includes you and me and everyone else. If that isn't true, it's no wonder that we basically lost interest.

Easter is the feast of hope, direction, purpose, meaning, and community. We're all in this together. The cynicism and negativity that our country and many other countries have descended into show a clear example of what happens when people do not have hope. If it's all hopeless, we individually lose hope too. Easter is the announcement of a common hope. When we sing in the Easter hymn that Christ has destroyed death, that means the death of all of us. It's not just about Jesus; it's to humanity that God promises, 'Life is not ended, it merely changes,' as we say in the funeral liturgy. That's what happened in Jesus, and that's what will happen in us. In the end, everything will be all right. History is set on an inherently positive and hopeful tangent.

Adapted from 'Everything Will Be All Right
in the End', Richard Rohr (homily, 21 April 2019)

God of resurrection,
of life, death, rebirth,
renew our hearts and minds.

God of promise,
of all beginnings and endings,
renew our hearts and minds.

God of hope,
of new growth and harvest,
renew our hearts and minds.

SATURDAY

Christian prays within us

N*ow there were some Greeks among those who went up to worship at the festival. They came to Philip, who was from Bethsaida in Galilee, with a request. 'Sir,' they said, 'we would like to see Jesus.' Philip went to tell Andrew; Andrew and Philip in turn told Jesus.*

Jesus replied, 'The hour has come for the Son of Man to be glorified. Very truly I tell you, unless a grain of wheat falls to the ground and dies, it remains only a single seed. But if it dies, it produces many seeds. Anyone who loves their life will lose it, while anyone who hates their life in this world will keep it for eternal life. Whoever serves me must follow me; and where I am, my servant also will be. My Father will honour the one who serves me . . .'

John 12:20–6

The practice of silent prayer rests on the resurrection mystery, that Christ has made a place for us; we could not make very much sense of the distinctly Christian understanding of contemplation without that resurrection dimension. There are, of course, plenty of techniques and traditions in the religions of the world that value contemplation or meditation in silence, and from many of them we can learn (and I have learned a huge amount from them myself). But for us to make something like *Christian* sense of it all, we need that Trinitarian perspective, grounded in the resurrection. When I come before God in silence, I come before God allowing the Holy Spirit to put Christ's words into my mouth, to let my breath be breathed anew in the Spirit, carrying the words of Christ, and just let the Trinity be where I am when I pray.

We could not make much sense of such a practice without belief in the resurrection, without the belief that Christ, having passed from death to life, belongs now in God's eternity. As one French theologian put it, 'Jesus is tipped over into the eternal life of God.' Standing eternally before God: holding our place there before God, so that where he is we may be also (John 12:26). Prayer does not have to be an attempt to get God's attention, not an action we perform on God all the time, but the action God desires to perform in us to bring us to life. And when people are faced with great anxieties about their prayer life, it can at times be of great importance to say to them, 'Prayer is also letting God be God.' And if you're feeling that you're exhausting yourself with the endless effort to concentrate properly, to get from here to there (wherever 'there' is) you may very well need to hear the good news that prayer is also God being God in you, if you let him ... prayer is not something we squeeze out with effort, but something that happens when we let God be God.

From *God with Us*, Rowan Williams

*B*reathe on me, Breath of God,
  fill me with life anew,
that I may love what thou dost love,
and do what thou wouldst do.

Breathe on me, Breath of God,
until my heart is pure,
until with thee I will one will
to do and to endure.

Breathe on me, Breath of God,
till I am wholly thine,
until this earthly part of me
glows with the fire divine.

Breathe on me, Breath of God,
so shall I never die,
but live with thee the perfect life
of thine eternity.

Edwin Hatch (1835–89)

FOURTH WEEK
OF EASTER

FOURTH SUNDAY OF EASTER

Love stronger than death

God is our refuge and strength,
a very present help in trouble;
therefore we will not fear, though the earth be moved
and though the mountains be toppled
into the depths of the sea;
though the waters rage and foam,
and though the mountains tremble at its tumult.
The Lord of hosts is with us,
the God of Jacob is our stronghold.
There is a river whose streams make glad the city of God,
the holy habitation of the Most High.
God is in the midst of her;
she shall not be overthrown;
God shall help her at the break of day.
The Lord of hosts is with us,
the God of Jacob is our stronghold.

Psalm 46:1–8, *The Revised Psalter*

Easter morning ... After the Gospel we spoke together about the resurrection. Liz, who works with many anguished people, said, 'We have to keep rolling away the large stones that prevent people from coming out of their graves.' Elizabeth, who lives with four handicapped people in a L'Arche foyer, said, 'After the resurrection Jesus had breakfast again with his friends and showed them the importance of the small, ordinary things of life.' Sue, who is wondering whether she might be called to go to Honduras and work with the L'Arche community there, said, 'It is such a comfort to know that Jesus' wounds remain visible in his risen body. Our wounds are not taken away, but become sources of hope to others.'

As everyone spoke, I felt very close to the Easter event. It was not a spectacular event forcing people to believe. Rather, it was an event for the friends of Jesus, for those who had known him, listened to him, and believed in him. It was a very intimate event: a word here, a gesture there, and a gradual awareness that something new was being born – small, hardly noticed, but with the potential to change the face of the earth. Mary of Magdala heard her name. John and Peter saw the empty grave. Jesus' friends felt their hearts burn in encounters that find expression in the remarkable words 'He is risen.' All had remained the same, while all had changed.

The five of us, sitting in a circle around the table with a little bread and a little wine, speaking softly about the way we were recognizing him in our lives, knew deep in our hearts that for us too all had changed, while all had remained the same. Our struggles are not ended. On Easter morning we can still feel the pains of our family and friends, the pains of our hearts. They are still there and will be there for a long time. Still, all is different because we have met Jesus and he has spoken to us.

There was a simple, quiet joy among us and a deep sense of being loved by a love that is stronger, much stronger, than death.

From *The Road to Daybreak*, Henri J. M. Nouwen

G racious God,
bringer of light and life,
we praise you
for the light of new life in Jesus.
For the light that shone on
Mary Magdalene,
Simon Peter,
John, the beloved disciple,
and all the witnesses of your resurrection.

We pray that the Easter light
may shine on us
and lighten the darkness
of all who are wounded or broken
or fearful
in the world of today:
that they may know they are loved
by a love that is stronger than death.

MONDAY

Signs of hope

'*Do not let your hearts be troubled. You believe in God; believe also in me. My Father's house has many rooms; if that were not so, would I have told you that I am going there to prepare a place for you? And if I go and prepare a place for you, I will come back and take you to be with me that you also may be where I am. You know the way to the place where I am going.'*

Thomas said to him, 'Lord, we don't know where you are going, so how can we know the way?'

Jesus answered, 'I am the way and the truth and the life. No one comes to the Father except through me. If you really know me, you will know my Father as well. From now on, you do know him and have seen him.'

John 14:1–7

Does Christianity make a difference? ... It invites us to a way of life that should be puzzling, intriguing. In a world which has lost its utopias we should be a sign of hope; we are invited to embrace the radical freedom of Christ and to enjoy even now some foretaste of the happiness for which we are made. If these qualities are not found among us, then it may be because we are afraid. We fear to embark on the pilgrimage to God. In *Pilgrim's Progress* Despondency explains that it was 'slavish fears' that kept himself and his daughter Much-afraid from the journey. 'For to be plain with you, they are ghosts, which we entertained when we first began to be Pilgrims and could never shake them off after. And they walk about and seek Entertainment of the Pilgrims, but for our sakes, shut ye doors upon them.' It is fear that may prevent us from enjoying the full freedom of giving our lives away, knowing that we may be hurt. The angel appears to the women at the empty tomb and says, 'Do not be afraid', but it was fear that blinded the women to the meaning of the empty tomb, so that they said nothing ... We cannot be convincing witnesses to the gospel unless we are inhabited by an inexplicable courage.

From *What is the Point of Being a Christian?*, Timothy Radcliffe

*L*ord, the Way, the Truth and the Life,
    the bringer of hope to a weary world:
may we know you as the Way to the Father,
may we believe in you as our Risen Lord
and may we trust you to be alongside us
as we walk this earthly journey
with faith and courage.

TUESDAY

The reality of Jesus

'*Come, let us return to the LORD.
He has torn us to pieces
but he will heal us;
he has injured us
but he will bind up our wounds.
After two days he will revive us;
on the third day he will restore us,
that we may live in his presence.
Let us acknowledge the LORD;
let us press on to acknowledge him.
As surely as the sun rises,
he will appear;
he will come to us like the winter rains,
like the spring rains that water the earth.*'

Hosea 6:1–3

We must seek the truth wherever we find it. I am a traditionalist and yet I also sit in awe when I listen to all of the brilliant people that God has produced, whether I'm sitting at the feet of an outstanding theologian or listening to an outstanding scientist. When religious truth, scientific truth, and whatever truth come together and become part of the framework that makes sense of the universe, I am awestruck, and I find that truth then has a self-authenticating authority.

Jesus, both as we read about him in the New Testament and as we envision him as a role model for our own lives, can help Christians to know how God wants us to live. But here too we must be careful how we read the accounts of his life. I am foursquare in the Catholic faith that is enshrined in our prayer books, in our formularies, in the creeds. But when we say Jesus Christ is ascended into heaven, you don't believe that he got into a kind of ecclesiastical lift that took him into the stratosphere. This is language that is being used figuratively because the realities that are being described are not human realities, they are supernatural realities. When we speak even about the resurrection of Jesus Christ, it is not the revivification of a corpse. It is speaking about a tremendous reality: that Jesus Christ is risen, his life is real, he is accessible to me in Cape Town, as he is accessible to someone in Tokyo or New York or London or Sao Paulo or Sidney – that Jesus Christ is someone whose life makes a difference to me and to so many others two thousand years after he lived.

From *God Has a Dream*, Desmond Tutu

*L*ord, sometimes I'm puzzled
and I ask: Where are you?

A cloud seems to hide you from my sight.
I am more conscious of your absence
than your presence.

But the truth is that you are here;
with me, alongside me, within me.
This is no dream, no make-believe.
This is for real: you are in the here and now
of this day, in this place.
Lord, I believe!

WEDNESDAY

Joy made possible

*R*ejoice in the Lord always. I will say it again: rejoice! Let your gentleness be evident to all. The Lord is near. Do not be anxious about anything, but in every situation, by prayer and petition, with thanksgiving, present your requests to God.

Philippians 4:4–6

Joy is about discovering the world is more than you ever suspected, and so that you yourself are more than you suspected. The joy of the resurrection has a unique place in Christian faith and imagination because this event breaks open the shell of the world we thought we knew and projects us into the new and mysterious realm in which victorious mercy and inexhaustible love make the rules. And because it is the revelation of something utterly basic about reality itself, it is a joy that cannot just be at the mercy of passing feelings. It roots itself in the heart and remains as a foundation for everything else. The Christian is not therefore the person who has accepted a particular set of theories about the universe but the person who lives by the power of the joy that is laid bare in the event of the resurrection of Jesus. To be baptized 'into' Christ is to be given a lasting connection with joy, a channel through which the basic sense of being where we ought to be can always come through, however much we choke it up with selfishness and worry. Sometimes, clearing out the debris needs a bit of explosive – encounter with an extraordinary person or story, experience of passionate love, witnessing profound suffering, whatever shakes us out of our so-called 'normal' habits. But we can at least contribute to this by giving time to clearing the channel as best we may, in silence, in the space of reflection. And we can also ask persistently what it is in our social environment that will most help to create this for others, especially those who live with constant anxiety, because of poverty, disability or other sorts of disadvantage.

Christian joy, the joy of Easter, is offered to the world not to guarantee a permanently happy society in the sense of a society free from tension, pain or disappointment, but to affirm that whatever happens in the unpredictable world – sometimes wonderfully, sometimes horribly unpredictable – there is a deeper level of reality, a world within the world, where love and reconciliation are ceaselessly at work, a world with which contact can be made so that we are able to live honestly and courageously with the challenges constantly thrown at us. As on the first Easter morning, it is as if 'the fountains of the great deep' are broken open, and we are allowed to see, like Peter and John at the empty tomb, into the darkness for a moment – and find our world turned upside down, joy made possible.

From Rowan Williams' sermon at Canterbury Cathedral, Easter 2011

*S*ing choirs of heaven! Let saints and angels sing!
Around God's throne exult in harmony.
Now Jesus Christ is risen from the grave.
Salute your King in glorious symphony.

Sing choirs of earth! Behold, your light has come!
The glory of the Lord shines radiantly.
Lift up your hearts, for Christ has conquered death.
The night is past; the day of life is here.

Sing Church of God! Exult with joy outpoured!
The gospel trumpets tell of victory won.
Your Saviour lives: he's with you evermore.
Let all God's people shout the long Amen.

Found in *Common Praise*, 156

THURSDAY

'Some doubted'

*T**hen the eleven disciples went to Galilee, to the mountain where
Jesus had told them to go. When they saw him, they worshipped
him; but some doubted. Then Jesus came to them and said, 'All
authority in heaven and on earth has been given to me. Therefore go
and make disciples of all nations, baptising them in the name of the
Father and of the Son and of the Holy Spirit, and teaching them to
obey everything I have commanded you. And surely I am with you
always, to the very end of the age.'*

Matthew 28:16–20

The exams have been completed, the training is done, the skills have been honed and learnt and now you can set off and begin this new chapter. It is a stage in life that has been repeated and repeated down the centuries albeit in different situations and contexts. A person, whether young or old, spends some time learning a new set of skills and eventually there comes the time when they set off to put all they have learnt into practice. It is an exciting and nerve wracking time and one of those watershed moments in any person's life.

The disciples have spent a long time in preparation with Christ learning and listening and following and now they are commissioned to carry on the work, and it is interesting that even at this stage we are told that 'some doubted'. Despite the resurrection appearances, not to mention all that they had seen and heard during Christ's ministry, there are still doubts lingering in the air. In many ways I am glad that they are present as it is a very human response and an almost universal human trait to harbour doubts. Doubts about ourselves or others, doubts about the present or future, doubts about what is really true.

It seems to me that doubt in itself can become a vital part of what it means to be a follower of Christ. Doubt properly expressed and acted upon can become the stimulus and spark for a life that continues to be open to the renewing and cleansing power of the Holy One. Doubt is not the same as passivity, and we should remember that those who doubted still turned up on the mountain. The doubt itself only becomes destructive when it begins to convince us of the lie that we are alone.

Christ proclaims to the disciples; to all those present, the honest doubters and the humble worshippers, 'I am with you always, to the very end of the age.' The Commission then is not simply a Commission of doing but also of being. We are commissioned into the truth that there will be no place or time; no condition or context when we will be alone. And so we seek to live day by day exploring the radical nature of that resurrection truth.

Brother Jonathan, Stations of the Resurrection
No. 11, at Mucknell Abbey, on 31 May 2022

*C*hrist, our Lord,
  risen from the dead,
come and enter into the darkness of our doubt and despair
with the bright light of your presence.
Help us never to give up,
but to persevere
and put our trust in the power of your resurrection,
that we may rejoice in you the Risen Lord, our Saviour,
who lives and reigns with the Father and the Holy Spirit,
one God, world without end. Amen.

FRIDAY

Prayer and the cross

*B*ut *whatever were gains to me I now consider loss for the sake of Christ. What is more, I consider everything a loss because of the surpassing worth of knowing Christ Jesus my Lord, for whose sake I have lost all things. I consider them garbage, that I may gain Christ and be found in him, not having a righteousness of my own that comes from the law, but that which is through faith in Christ – the righteousness that comes from God on the basis of faith. I want to know Christ – yes, to know the power of his resurrection and participation in his sufferings, becoming like him in his death, and so, somehow, attaining to the resurrection from the dead.*

Philippians 3:7–11

In Paul's experience the resurrection is never without the cross; the glory of the one is made possible by and finds its meaning in the suffering of the other. When Paul is reviewing his ambitions for the future in Philippians, he says that he wants to share in both the agony and the victory of Jesus: 'I want to know Christ and the power of his resurrection, and the sharing of his suffering by becoming like him in his death, if somehow I may attain the resurrection from the dead' (Philippians 3:10–11). Such a spirituality embraces not only triumph but also failure, not only the revealed glory of a manifestly present God but days when that God appears to have turned away his face and dire and deadly things have their way with us as they did with Jesus on the cross.

If Ephesians and its boundless expectations lie at one end of the Pauline spectrum, 2 Corinthians with its picture of an apostle beset with difficulties and threatened by abandonment lies at the other: 'We are afflicted in every way but not crushed; perplexed, but not driven to despair; persecuted, but not forsaken; struck down but not destroyed; always carrying in the body the death of Jesus, so that the life of Jesus may also be made visible in our bodies' (2 Corinthians 4:8–10). That sounds like a Christian experience more akin to our own, hoping for the power of the resurrection to manifest itself amidst a life burdened by the failure and perplexity of the cross.

From *Praying with Paul*, Tom Smail

*D raw me whether through love or grief,
draw me through bitterness or sweetness,
through adversity or prosperity,
through ways narrow or broad,
through things easy or hard.*

*Draw me through what and with what you will,
so that I have you only in my life
and all my hope is here and in the future,
that I may never be separated from the fire of your love,
because you are all I desire.*

SATURDAY

The community of the Risen Lord

They devoted themselves to the apostles' teaching and to fellowship, to the breaking of bread and to prayer. Everyone was filled with awe at the many wonders and signs performed by the apostles. All the believers were together and had everything in common. They sold property and possessions to give to anyone who had need. Every day they continued to meet together in the temple courts. They broke bread in their homes and ate together with glad and sincere hearts, praising God and enjoying the favour of all the people. And the Lord added to their number daily those who were being saved.

Acts 2:42–7

In the book of Acts St Luke describes the first Christians as keeping together in the teaching, in the fellowship, in the breaking of bread, and in the prayers. It is the situation foreshadowed at Emmaus. The teaching is Jesus' opening to them the scriptures. The fellowship is their oneness, their hearts burning within them as he talked with them by the way. The prayers are this basic posture of Christian affection and need – 'Stay with us', which is a way of saying 'Lord, have mercy upon us', or, 'the grace of our Lord Jesus Christ be with us all'. The breaking of bread is explicitly there ...

Christian faith comes and grows as you take your place responsibly within the fellowship, the teaching, the prayer and the sacramental life, and the pain and perplexity of the Church of Christ.

This is not to say that there is any easy way to faith in the risen Christ. All of the disciples came to their individual moment of recognition after much perplexity. And when they knew him it was not a mere recognition that it was Jesus, it was that perception in depth that activated their memory, the hints left in the mind as they had struggled all the way through to understand life, and all the hope and love that had been gathering round the image of Jesus. The cumulative result of all this was that at last they saw him as the Lord.

From *Five for Sorrow, Ten for Joy*, J. Neville Ward

The cross
 We shall take it
The Bread
We shall break it
The pain
We shall bear it
The joy
We shall share it
The gospel
We shall live it
The love
We shall give it
The light
We shall cherish it
The darkness
God shall perish it.
Amen.

From *God's Family at Worship*, Council of Churches for Wales

FIFTH WEEK OF EASTER

FIFTH SUNDAY OF EASTER

The nearness of God

*H*e said to them, 'This is what I told you while I was still with you: everything must be fulfilled that is written about me in the Law of Moses, the Prophets and the Psalms.'

Then he opened their minds so they could understand the Scriptures. He told them, 'This is what is written: the Messiah will suffer and rise from the dead on the third day, and repentance for the forgiveness of sins will be preached in his name to all nations, beginning at Jerusalem. You are witnesses of these things . . .'

Luke 24:44–8

They [the disciples] were not ready then to follow where he was going. They were too confused and trapped. He must have known long before that he would have to endure the ordeal uniquely and alone. And they for their part had to face this most glaring proof, not only that he had never been the Messiah they had envisaged, but also that they had never been the pioneers of the Kingdom he had tried to make them. Yet after that disastrous, God-forsaken debacle, very soon after, they knew he was more alive than ever, closer to God and yet present to them as never before. He who had shown God to them now showed himself to them, and from that time they would never think of God without thinking of him. To proclaim the Kingdom of God was to proclaim Jesus. Their certainty of his exaltation by God, which was also a certainty of his presence in their midst, convinced them that his knowledge of God as Father had been true, his representation of the Father in his words and behaviour had been true, his message that a new age of God's rule was about to break in had been fulfilled, his defiance in setting himself above certain customs and his disturbing acceptance of outsiders and outcasts was confirmed, and even his decision to let himself be handed over to helplessness, apparent failure and death was truly vindicated. By raising him from death into glory God acknowledged it all. The one who had called people to believe had become the object of faith, and to decide for or against God's rule was identical with a decision for or against Jesus. Thinking about Jesus and thinking about God had become inseparable. Their sense of his nearness, though invisible, was like their sense of God's nearness. And this original conviction of those who experienced the resurrection appearances seemed strangely transmissible, so that others who never knew him 'in the flesh' were as profoundly affected by the story told to them as the immediate companions of Jesus had been by his resurrection.

From *The Christlike God*, John V. Taylor

Walk beside us, Risen Lord,
  when we are puzzled and confused,
when we are disappointed and fail to understand.

Walk beside us, Risen Lord,
when we meet the unfamiliar and the new,
when we lack faith and hope
and are full of fear.

Walk beside us Risen Lord,
and make yourself known
in the broken bread
and the Word of Life.

Walk beside us, Risen Lord,
along the path
that leads to the future
and be with us always.

MONDAY

A little while . . .

*J*esus went on to say, 'In a little while you will see me no more, and then after a little while you will see me.'
At this, some of his disciples said to one another, 'What does he mean by saying, "In a little while you will see me no more, and then after a little while you will see me," and "Because I am going to the Father"?' They kept asking, 'What does he mean by "a little while"? We don't understand what he is saying.'

Jesus saw that they wanted to ask him about this, so he said to them, 'Are you asking one another what I meant when I said, "In a little while you will see me no more, and then after a little while you will see me"? Very truly I tell you, you will weep and mourn while the world rejoices. You will grieve, but your grief will turn to joy. A woman giving birth to a child has pain because her time has come; but when her baby is born she forgets the anguish because of her joy that a child is born into the world. So with you: now is your time of grief, but I will see you again and you will rejoice, and no one will take away your joy . . .'

John 16:16–22

When the disciples asked Christ to explain his departure and return, he did not explain the nature of these mysterious events, but he stated the principle or purpose of them. No birth, he says, is without the pains of travail, but the birth of a child is well worth the pains. Unless we agonise at some time over the birth of faith, faith is not ours, it is not a personal possession, it is not the child of our own soul. Christ leaves his disciples so far and so long as is required for the pains of their travail. It is not an act of desertion on his part, but a merciful providence. Darkness and uncertainty, loneliness and spiritual effort are necessary to us, and, taken right, they are the growth of faith. They are as much the gifts of God as certainty and comfort. A little while, he says, and I will see you again, and your heart shall rejoice: your joy no man taketh from you.

From *The Crown of the Year*, Austin Farrer

L ord, in all the uncertainties of life
help us to put our trust in you.
Give us the faith to know
that in times of trial you never depart from us
but remain with us always.
Turn our heaviness into joy
and clothe us with gladness and rejoicing
that we may give thanks to you for ever.

TUESDAY

Access to God

We have this hope as an anchor for the soul, firm and secure. It enters the inner sanctuary behind the curtain, where our fore-runner, Jesus, has entered on our behalf. He has become a high priest for ever, in the order of Melchizedek.

Hebrews 6:19–20

With a loud cry, Jesus breathed his last. The curtain of the temple was torn in two from top to bottom.

Mark 15:37–8

The curtain referred to here, is the curtain in the Temple in Jerusalem that separated the Holy of Holies from the rest of the Temple. In this strictly hierarchical building, only certain people can enter certain places. They need to ritually cleanse themselves first and offer proper sacrifices; and only the High Priest, and then only once a year, on the Day of the Passover, and appropriately dressed and appropriately prepared, can enter the Holy of Holies, behind the curtain of separation, taking with him the blood of the sacrifice. His job is to make peace with God. Or so it was believed.

This is what the Temple in Jerusalem was for. It was a place where sacrifices were offered, and where atonement was made with God. And it involved a lot of blood and a lot of death. Sacrifices were offered day after day and year after year. The whole place would have been filled with the howls of death and the stench of blood.

It is this curtain which is torn down. And it is torn down at the precise moment that Jesus dies on the cross. As the letter to the Hebrews puts it, Jesus our Great High Priest 'enters once for all into the Holy Place, not with the blood of goats and calves, but with his own blood . . . for this reason he is the mediator of a new covenant' (Hebrews 9:12, 15).

And the holy place he enters is not the Temple in Jerusalem, but heaven itself. This is what Easter is all about. Christ who laid down his life on the cross, which seemed to us on Good Friday so tragic and bereft, is now raised to glory. Mary Magdalen stood in the dawning light of the first Easter Day and beheld Christ; not a resuscitated corpse, not a fleeting ghost, but the first piece of the new creation, the one whose life is lived in our life and who by his death and resurrection carries our humanity to the highest heaven and paves the way to glory. He doesn't go into the Temple, because he is the Temple! It is in him and through him that we now have access to God. On Easter morning it is as if God himself hangs up a sign on the Temple door saying 'Closed. By order of the management. What you once purchased here is now available for free through the death and resurrection of Jesus Christ'. And that's why we don't want notices in church saying that some bits are more holy than others and belong to some people more than the rest. There is no citizenship or passport control around the font. There is no fence around the altar. All are welcome.

Brothers and sisters, the stone has been rolled away, the veil of the Temple has been torn in two, Christ is risen and we are called to live to reflect this new reality in the lives we lead, which is why race hatred, homophobia, prejudice, intolerance, war and violence have no place in the kingdom of God. As St Paul puts it, writing to the church in Ephesus: Christ 'has broken down the dividing wall that was the hostility between us . . . through him we have access to God' (Ephesians 2:14, 18). This is the meaning of the resurrection. It is the Easter joy, Christ's story, that we must live and share in the world.

From Stephen Cottrell's online sermon for York Diocese, Easter 2022

L ord Jesus Christ,
  you have come to us,
born as one of us,
Mary's Son;
led out to die on Calvary,
risen from death to set us free,
living Lord Jesus, help us see
you are Lord.

Lord Jesus Christ,
I would come to you,
live my life for you,
Son of God.
All your commands I know are true,
your many gifts will make me new,
into my life your power breaks through,
living Lord.

Patrick Appleford

WEDNESDAY

The new life in Jesus

*F*or God, who said, 'Let light shine out of darkness,' made his
light shine in our hearts to give us the light of the knowledge of
God's glory displayed in the face of Christ.

*But we have this treasure in jars of clay to show that this all-
surpassing power is from God and not from us. We are hard pressed
on every side, but not crushed; perplexed, but not in despair; persecuted, but not abandoned; struck down, but not destroyed. We always
carry around in our body the death of Jesus, so that the life of Jesus
may also be revealed in our body. For we who are alive are always
being given over to death for Jesus' sake, so that his life may also be
revealed in our mortal body. So then, death is at work in us, but life
is at work in you.*

2 Corinthians 4:6–12

To accept death as an act of love is not easy, and I believe that this was the climax of Christ's achievement in his travail towards love ... And it is for us to imitate him, even in our weakness.

Real death is separation from God, and this is unbearable, real death is faithlessness, hopelessness, lovelessness.

We all know what pain and sadness are, for we have all experienced them and are all immersed in them ...

Real death is emptiness, darkness, desolation, despair, hatred, destruction. So ... Christ agreed to enter into this death, into this separation, so as to identify himself with all who were in separation, and to save them.

When he was immersed in their darkness, he made brightness of truth burst forth with his resurrection.

When engulfed in the abyss of their lovelessness he showed them the infinite joy of love with his resurrection,

By rising from the dead, Christ made all things new.

By rising from the dead he opened new heavens.

By rising from the dead he opened new life.

From *Blessed Are You Who Believed*, Carlo Carretto

*R*isen Christ, when darkness overwhelms us
may your dawn beckon.

When fear paralyses us
may your touch release us.

When grief torments us
may your peace enfold us.

When memories haunt us
may your presence heal us.

When apathy stagnates us
may your challenge renew us.

When courage leaves us
may your spirit inspire us.

When despair grips us
may your hope restore us.

And when death threatens us
may your resurrection light lead us.

Annabel Shilson-Thomas/CAFOD

THURSDAY

'Follow me'

*T*he third time he said to him, 'Simon son of John, do you love me?'

Peter was hurt because Jesus asked him the third time, 'Do you love me?' He said, 'Lord, you know all things; you know that I love you.'

Jesus said, 'Feed my sheep. Very truly I tell you, when you were younger you dressed yourself and went where you wanted; but when you are old you will stretch out your hands, and someone else will dress you and lead you where you do not want to go.' Jesus said this to indicate the kind of death by which Peter would glorify God. Then he said to him, 'Follow me!'

John 21:17–19

'*Follow me*'. A few days before the Lord had said *Whither you go thou canst not follow me now, but thou shalt follow afterwards (John 13:36)*. Now He says '*Follow me*'. For it is possible now. The outward presence of the Lord is being withdrawn; the power of the Holy Spirit is given and will soon take possession; Peter, reckless and cowardly by turns, fighting in the garden but denying in the High Priest's court, will stand forth before the rulers of his people in the serenity of imperturbable courage – Rock-man indeed.

Yet it is with reference, not to what he will do, but what others will do to him, that the Lord says with so solemn an emphasis *Follow me*. Is it not true that in a certain deep sense nothing which the Lord did was so important as what others did to Him? No doubt His endurance is what gave its quality to the event; but His passivity is more powerful than His acts. He reigns from the Tree. Will Peter follow to the end?

Yes, to the very bitter end; yet even so, if the legend is trustworthy, there lingered to the end some of the old weakness which makes Peter so unfailing a spring of encouragement to most of us. The example of Paul is of little use to me; I am not a hero. The example of John is but of little more use; my love is so feeble. But Peter is a source of constant encouragement, for his weakness is manifest, yet because he was truly the friend of his Lord he became the Prince of the Apostles and glorified God by his death.

From *Readings in St John's Gospel*, William Temple

*L*iving God, the wellspring of life,
  *pour into our hearts the living water
of your grace.
By your light we see light.
Increase our faith
and grant that we may walk in
the brightness of your presence,
following Jesus Christ, our Risen Lord.*

FRIDAY

The miracle of the resurrection

For what I received I passed on to you as of first importance: that Christ died for our sins according to the Scriptures, that he was buried, that he was raised on the third day according to the Scriptures, and that he appeared to Cephas, and then to the Twelve. After that, he appeared to more than five hundred of the brothers and sisters at the same time, most of whom are still living, though some have fallen asleep. Then he appeared to James, then to all the apostles, and last of all he appeared to me also, as to one abnormally born.

For I am the least of the apostles and do not even deserve to be called an apostle, because I persecuted the church of God. But by the grace of God I am what I am, and his grace to me was not without effect. No, I worked harder than all of them — yet not I, but the grace of God that was with me. Whether, then, it is I or they, this is what we preach, and this is what you believed.

1 Corinthians 15:3–11

In the earliest days of Christianity an 'apostle' was first and foremost a man who claimed to be an eyewitness of the Resurrection. Only a few days after the Crucifixion when two candidates were nominated for the vacancy created by the treachery of Judas, their qualification was that they had known Jesus personally both before and after His death and could offer first hand evidence of the Resurrection in addressing the outer world (Acts 1:22) . . .

When modern writers talk of the Resurrection, they usually mean one particular moment – the discovery of the Empty Tomb and the appearance of Jesus a few yards away from it. The story of that moment is what Christian apologists now chiefly try to support and sceptics chiefly try to impugn. But this most exclusive concentration on the first five minutes or so of the Resurrection would have astonished the earliest Christian teachers. In claiming to have seen the Resurrection they were not necessarily claiming to have seen *that*. Some of them had, some of them had not. It had no more importance than any of the other appearances of the risen Jesus – apart from the poetic and dramatic importance which the beginning of things must always have. What they were claiming was that they had all, at one time or another, met Jesus during the six or seven weeks that followed His death. Sometimes they seem to have been alone when they did so, but on one occasion twelve of them saw Him together, and on another occasion about five hundred of them. St Paul says that the majority of the five hundred were still alive when he wrote the First Letter to the Corinthians, i.e. in about AD 55.

From *Miracles*, C. S. Lewis

R isen Lord, light of the world,
who on the third day rose again from the dead,
come, stand among us now:
dispel the darkness of night
with your celestial brightness,
that we may walk before you as in the day,
and as children of light;
to the glory of your name,
our Risen Lord.

SATURDAY

Failure and forgiveness

*B*ut God raised him from the dead, and for many days he was
seen by those who had travelled with him from Galilee to
Jerusalem. They are now his witnesses to our people. We tell you the
good news: what God promised our ancestors he has fulfilled for us,
their children, by raising up Jesus ... Therefore, my friends, I want
you to know that through Jesus the forgiveness of sins is proclaimed
to you. Through him everyone who believes is set free from every sin,
a justification you were not able to obtain under the law of Moses.*

Acts 13:30–3, 38–9

In the days of Christ's Passover the community [of the disciples] had disintegrated; when the Shepherd was struck down the sheep were scattered. They were too terrified to stand by him, and during the next few days they were dragged through a series of shattering experiences: first shame and fear, then overwhelming grief and shock at his death, then emptiness and desolation, then bewilderment at confused tales from excited women of which they could make no sense. Then Jesus stood in their midst, saying, 'Peace'. No wonder they were dumbfounded.

He gathered them with no word of reproach and gave them the peace purchased by suffering. They were forgiven, lifted into his joy, and sent to preach forgiveness of sins to all nations (cf. Luke 24:46–8) . . .

Ever since that day, Christian community has been a place where people fail and are forgiven. It has been a place where the risen Christ stands among us, bearing the wounds of our failures as transfigured scars, and breathing into us the Spirit of the new creation.

We fail before God, and we fail God. We fail before one another, and we fail one another. If what we are living together is really a shared life in Christ, there must be room in it both for the experience of failure and for the recognition that it is in failure that the Easter mystery takes hold . . .

In bearing and being borne with, in forgiving and being forgiven, in accepting and affirming others and being accepted and affirmed ourselves, we know the Lord. In men and women as they are, sinful and weak and redeemed, still failing often but allowing Christ's compassion to flow freely among them: this is where Easter happens.

From *Gateway to Hope*, Sister Maria Boulding

*L*ord God, I know that this is a sick world
and that my sins and failures
are part of the sickness.
I also know that, though I do not deserve it,
Jesus, your Son, has died for my healing.
Through the crucified and risen love of Jesus,
I can come to you, Father,
and find forgiveness, peace and eternal life.

Stir in me the healing power of the Holy Spirit
for my own wholeness,
that I myself may be a channel of healing in the world,
in the Name of Jesus, the Prince of Peace.

SIXTH WEEK OF EASTER

SIXTH SUNDAY OF EASTER

The Lord is here!

*I*n him we were also chosen, having been predestined according to the plan of him who works out everything in conformity with the purpose of his will, in order that we, who were the first to put our hope in Christ, might be for the praise of his glory. And you also were included in Christ when you heard the message of truth, the gospel of your salvation. When you believed, you were marked in him with a seal, the promised Holy Spirit, who is a deposit guaranteeing our inheritance until the redemption of those who are God's possession – to the praise of his glory.

Ephesians 1:11–14

'Belief', in English, connotes gullibility, acceptance without proof. 'Belief' in the New Testament means much more than the English word can convey. Belief is knowing, but a knowing which is not based solely on observation, inner reasoning, logical deduction, or the assurance of other people. Belief is an inner sensing, more like intuition. We cannot create it, manufacture it, or force ourselves into it; all that we can do is be still and discover the gift within ourselves. 'The Spirit who lived in Jesus and raised him from the dead, now lives in us' (Romans 8:11). This is the reality in which we live. By praying the Gospel scenes imaginatively, we can meet the risen Christ now, living within us and amongst us, pledge of our resurrection ...

How reliable are the Gospel accounts? Was there really an empty tomb? Did Jesus really rise again from the dead? What kind of body did he have? If so, what kind of bodies will we have?

These are very interesting and important questions, but if we start with these questions and try to find satisfactory answers before praying the resurrection scenes, we shall never get started. Accept the resurrection narratives as they are presented in the Gospels, leaving these other questions aside for a moment. This is not intellectual dishonesty, but intellectual humility, an acknowledgement that the resurrection is a mystery into which God alone can lead us, a mystery in which we are now living. Stand with John at the empty tomb and pray to believe as he believed. Be with the other disciples in the upper room, listen to their fears and tell them of your own. See the risen Christ among you and hear him say to you, 'Peace', as he shows you his wounded hands and side. Imagination can put us in touch with the reality that Christ is

risen, that he is our peace. Be with Mary in the garden recognizing him in the gardener. Be with the two disciples on the
road to Emmaus and meet him in the stranger. Be still and
hear his Spirit in your heart calling you by name and saying,
'I am closer to you than you are to yourself. I shall never leave
you, for you and I are one undivided person.'

Then bring your attention back into the present and look
around.

The Lord is truly risen, is within us and amongst us,
alleluia!

From *Oh God, Why?*, Gerard W. Hughes

*L*ord God,
  help us to be honest with you
and with ourselves
as we look for answers to those questions
which arise within us.
Give us the faith to accept that as you,
our Risen Lord, were present to Mary, John, Peter
and the other disciples,
so you are alongside us now, calling us by name,
within us and around us.

MONDAY

Nothing is lost

*T*homas, sometimes called the Twin, one of the Twelve, was not with them when Jesus came. The other disciples told him, 'We have seen the Master.'

But he said, 'Unless I see the nail holes in his hands, put my finger in the nail holes, and stick my hand in his side, I won't believe it.' Eight days later the disciples were again in the room. This time Thomas was with them. Jesus came through the locked doors, stood among them, and said, 'Peace to you.'

Then he focused his attention on Thomas. 'Take your finger and examine my hands. Take your hand and stick it in my side. Don't be unbelieving. Believe.'

Thomas said, 'My Master! My God!'

Jesus said, 'So you believe because you've seen with your own eyes. Even better blessings are in store for those who believe without seeing.'

John 20:26–9, *The Message*

In a Christmas sermon, Eckhart, the medieval Dominican mystic, proposes the wonderful image of the Father giving birth to the Son eternally, but asks 'what does it avail me if this birth takes place unceasingly, but does not take place within myself?'

Christ is born in each one of us, unceasingly coming forth from the Father. My body, my emotions, my ideas, my actions, all can be the cradle of that birth. It is in the landscape of my own life that I can look to find the footsteps of the saviour.

The risen Christ, according to the Gospel of St John, invited Thomas 'the doubter' to probe the Lord's wounded hands, and even to place his own hand into Christ's opened side. The body, even the body of God, carries the history of our tragedies along with our triumphs. The glorified wounds are a powerful reminder that, whatever has happened to us along the way, even the damage, will become glorious, for from the opened side will living waters flow, but it is never lost. Although we step ultimately into the darkness, nothing is lost.

From *Crossing*, Mark Barrett OSB

R isen Lord, you reveal to us
    the love and radiance of the Father;
you bring to us the peace
that passes all understanding.
With you nothing is lost
for you came to save us.
We rejoice in your presence
and in the glory of your resurrection.
Strengthen our faith, Lord Jesus,
that we may know you live in eternity
with the Father and the Holy Spirit,
one God, world without end. Amen.

TUESDAY

A new life

*P*raise be to the God and Father of our Lord Jesus Christ! In his great mercy he has given us new birth into a living hope through the resurrection of Jesus Christ from the dead, and into an inheritance that can never perish, spoil or fade. This inheritance is kept in heaven for you, who through faith are shielded by God's power until the coming of the salvation that is ready to be revealed in the last time. In all this you greatly rejoice, though now for a little while you may have had to suffer grief in all kinds of trials. These have come so that the proven genuineness of your faith – of greater worth than gold, which perishes even though refined by fire – may result in praise, glory and honour when Jesus Christ is revealed. Though you have not seen him, you love him; and even though you do not see him now, you believe in him and are filled with an inexpressible and glorious joy, for you are receiving the end result of your faith, the salvation of your souls.*

1 Peter 1:3–9

In a very similar way to the writings of Paul, 1 Peter estab-lishes his theological premise, which includes the resurrec-tion, and then goes on to talk about the difference it makes – or should make – to the way in which we live our lives. This single sentence (1:3–12) is where Peter puts down the theo-logical foundations that underpin everything that he goes on to say about how we live our lives now. These opening few verses tell us something very important indeed about Peter's theology: very like Paul, he sees the whole of the Christian existence in the light of Jesus' resurrection ...

It's worth exploring the image Peter uses here. Paul describes our current existence using the image of dying and rising, drawn directly from the resurrection; Peter has a similar idea but brings in a different image – that of giving birth. One of the striking features of this passage is the verb that Peter uses to describe how it is that we have a new and living hope: he says that God has given birth to us again. On one level this is very familiar and it is like the image of being born again that we find in chapter 3 of St John's Gospel. What is unusual here is that the verb is active not passive, focused more on God than on us. The passage could have said that 'we have been born again by God' or 'brought to new life by God' but it does not. Instead it says that God gave birth to us again or regenerated us. God is not a distant contributor to new life but an active labourer as he brings us into the new realm of life in Christ.

Peter has made the link here between death and resurrec-tion, and birth. Having a baby is an experience akin to dying and rising again. At those times we stand right at the bounda-ries of life, and it can feel as though there is a hair's breadth between death and new life. It is this image that Peter chooses to use to describe what has happened to us as Christians. Through Jesus' resurrection God gives birth to us again. He recreates us into a hope that lives and breathes just as we do. The realm in which we now live is marked by living hope, not life-sapping despair. For the New Testament writers hope was not an emotion, as it often is today, but a reality. This living hope exists whether we feel hopeful or not and is another marker of the risen life we now live.

From *This Risen Existence*, Paula Gooder

B lessing and praise be to you,
  Lord and God and Father of our Lord Jesus Christ!
By your great mercy you have given us
new life and new hope
through the resurrection of our Lord Jesus Christ
from the dead.
You have brought us into an inheritance
that is imperishable, undefiled and unfading.
To you be praise, through Jesus Christ our Risen Lord,
who is alive and reigns with you and the Holy Spirit,
one God now and for ever. Amen.

WEDNESDAY EVE OF THE ASCENSION

From disciples to apostles

We are witnesses of everything he did in the country of the Jews and in Jerusalem. They killed him by hanging him on a cross, but God raised him from the dead on the third day and caused him to be seen. He was not seen by all the people, but by witnesses whom God had already chosen – by us who ate and drank with him after he rose from the dead. He commanded us to preach to the people and to testify that he is the one whom God appointed as judge of the living and the dead. All the prophets testify about him that everyone who believes in him receives forgiveness of sins through his name.

Acts 10:39–43

For one brief verse of the Gospel account it sounds as if everything really is back to normal: almost comically, after the horror of Good Friday and the bewilderment of the empty tomb, John tells us that 'they all went back to their own homes'. It is hard for us who have read the next chapter to recapture the first Easter, when they still knew nothing of the ascension or Pentecost. For all they now realized, the events of that Passover weekend had just been a hiccup. Jesus was back, life would carry on as before.

But no: even while appearing to them in bodily form, Jesus would never merely indulge his followers with the sunshine of his rediscovered presence. He was teaching them to let go of him, to see and feel him in a new way, to 'internalize' the relationship. They couldn't hold on to him in their company any more than the authorities could hold him down in the tomb. He was converting them from disciples into apostles, preparing them for their final and irrevocable sending-out in his name. The ascension was a second bereavement, but they had to go through it to receive the 'second blessing' of Pentecost. 'Don't be amazed, but go,' says the angel to the women; 'don't cling on to me, go,' says Jesus to Mary Magdalene; and in every one of his farewell stories there is this same refusal of cosiness, this insistence that from now on they, the disciples, are to play his part: 'as the Father has sent me, even so I send you'; 'you shall be my witnesses'.

And, as Acts and Paul make clear, this was understood in a radical sense: they had not just been commissioned as Jesus' deputies or delegates, but as his very Body, filled with his very Holy Spirit.

From *Bread of the World*, John Hadley

*R*isen Lord,
how good it is to be in your presence,
to know that you are alongside me
and that you will never leave me or forsake me.
Rejoicing in your risen life,
I accept the challenge
not only of being a disciple,
but also of being an apostle,
sent into the world to work
for justice, peace and reconciliation;
to be a bringer of hope
and an instrument of your love.

ASCENSION

FEAST OF THE ASCENSION

The new creation

*T*hen they gathered round him and asked him, 'Lord, are you at this time going to restore the kingdom to Israel?'

He said to them: 'It is not for you to know the times or dates the Father has set by his own authority. But you will receive power when the Holy Spirit comes on you; and you will be my witnesses in Jerusalem, and in all Judea and Samaria, and to the ends of the earth.'

After he said this, he was taken up before their very eyes, and a cloud hid him from their sight.

They were looking intently up into the sky as he was going, when suddenly two men dressed in white stood beside them. 'Men of Galilee,' they said, 'why do you stand here looking into the sky? This same Jesus, who has been taken from you into heaven, will come back in the same way you have seen him go into heaven.'

Acts 1:6–11

If Jesus is the presence of God's promise in our world, and if the Ascension means that, through the power of the resurrection, we now share the same calling as Jesus, seeing in his light and with his eyes, then two things follow. First, we as Christian believers are 'in heaven', but not so as to remove us from earth. Quite the contrary: in the middle of the world's life, we are given some share in God's perspective on things so that God through us may make his loving faithfulness real and effective here and now. And second, the things and persons of this world are seen in a new way, seen as charged with hope, with a future of glory and of healing. They are seen as if already part of the new heaven and new earth in which God's purposes have been brought to completion.

The Ascension celebrates the new creation, the bringing together of heaven and earth that has begun in the life of Jesus. When Jesus is seen no more in the old way, that does not mean he has abandoned the world, so that we must go and look for him outside it – 'looking up to the sky' like the disciples. His life is being lived in us: the new world is being brought to birth in us, gradually and sometimes painfully. We are caught up in the external movement of God's commitment to his creation. In and through Jesus we too have become a sign of promise. The light is on; the morning has come. The daystar from on high has dawned upon us.

From *Open to Judgement*, Rowan Williams

*L*ord,
  let this day
be a day of glory.

The glory of Bethlehem,
your coming to earth.
The glory of Cana,
your sharing our mirth.
The glory of Galilee,
your bringing of calm.
The glory of Bethesda,
your saving from harm.
The glory of Calvary,
your sacrificial love.
The glory of Easter,
your rising above.
The glory of Ascension,
your Presence to see.

Let this day
be a day of glory.

Adapted from *Tides and Seasons*, David Adam

FRIDAY AFTER THE ASCENSION

Living by faith

Therefore, if anyone is in Christ, the new creation has come: the old has gone, the new is here! All this is from God, who reconciled us to himself through Christ and gave us the ministry of reconciliation: that God was reconciling the world to himself in Christ, not counting people's sins against them. And he has committed to us the message of reconciliation. We are therefore Christ's ambassadors, as though God were making his appeal through us. We implore you on Christ's behalf: be reconciled to God. God made him who had no sin to be sin for us, so that in him we might become the righteousness of God.

1 Corinthians 5:17–21

The ascension of Christ seems to have been for the first Christians the spiritualization of religion. In the Easter story when Mary rushed forward to embrace Jesus in turmoil of excited recognition and love there is something odd about him. He who never held anyone at arm's length, who incessantly longed to communicate and share, says, 'Touch me not'.

We understand this to mean that Christ's presence with his friends was passing from the physical to the spiritual. The norm of Christian experience is not that of the first disciples who saw him, talked with him, ate with him, amused and annoyed him, but of those millions since who have not seen and yet have believed – never will see until that fulfilment that we cannot imagine except under such misty ideas as the coming of wholeness and the end of the partial.

We never come to the end of learning the meaning of this, that to live by faith is to have God but not, or only very rarely indeed, in the warm comfort of the feelings. What authenticates his presence is not any temporary emotional excitement but the slow freeing of our love so that we are able to express more of our self lovingly and have less need to withdraw or resist. It is a long term result; we shall have to wait a long time to be assured of it. For the time being, for now, faith is a cool affair; some would call it bleak, but one comes to like it so. Emotion is a tricky adjunct to religious experience, it easily makes fools of us unless it is the warmth of the mature and integrated person's response to life. What we want is meaning in our life, the drawing of the scattered and squandered self into a unity, less self-concern, more response to the next person, to beauty, to pain, to the fun of life, to reality. It is indeed God that we want.

From *Five for Sorrow, Ten for Joy*, J. Neville Ward

A lmighty God,
 you have made us for yourself
and our hearts are restless
till they find their rest in you:
teach us to offer ourselves to your service
that here we may have your peace
and in the world to come
may see you face to face;
through Jesus Christ our Lord. Amen.

St Augustine

SATURDAY AFTER THE ASCENSION

The blessing of the ascension

*W*hen he had led them out to the vicinity of Bethany, he lifted up his hands and blessed them. While he was blessing them, he left them and was taken up into heaven. Then they worshipped him and returned to Jerusalem with great joy. And they stayed continually at the temple, praising God.

Luke 24:50–3

L uke is aware that he needs to carry on the story and that he has to fill out that last picture of his Gospel in which the group of transformed disciples returned from the mountain of ascension to the temple, full of praise and worship. He retells the ascension story, correcting and filling in the details which are important for the future ...

We are not celebrating the absence of Jesus, for he is more truly present than ever he had been in the days of his mortal body, for by the Holy Spirit his promise is experienced: 'Where two or three are gathered in my name, I am there among them' (Matthew 19:20).

Nevertheless we are living in the 'time between' the first and second advent of our Lord Jesus. He is simply not here in any body or physical sense, and we have to live with a certain absence in our human and Christian experience ...

What was it, then, that gave the disciples such joy and energy when they descended Mount Olivet and returned to Jerusalem? We look back on those early days of the New Testament church and we are able to affirm the basis of our joy and hope. First, we are part of the living body of Christ, which is his Church on earth and in heaven. Second, that Church is sustained by his word in scripture and his presence in the Eucharist. Third, the same Holy Spirit who descended on the disciples at Pentecost indwells the Church and every believer today – enlightening and empowering. Fourth, with all these blessings we are called upon to proclaim the reconciling gospel in the world, and to live our lives of service and holiness, looking for and expecting the second advent of our Lord in glory. We must not indulge in speculating about dates or prophesying, but should live in the light of that coming and of the appearance of that kingdom in which Christ is called the Prince of Peace (Isaiah 9:8).

From *The Prayer Mountain*, Brother Ramon

R isen Lord of life and death:
help me to feel and know your presence
with me in my daily life,
and in the fellowship of your Church.

Grant me that sense of anticipation
of your second Advent
which filled the early disciples,
and let the Holy Spirit draw others to your love
manifested in my life. Amen.

SEVENTH WEEK
OF EASTER

SEVENTH SUNDAY OF EASTER (SUNDAY AFTER THE ASCENSION)

Coming and going

A fter the Lord Jesus had spoken to them, he was taken up into heaven and he sat at the right hand of God. Then the disciples went out and preached everywhere, and the Lord worked with them and confirmed his word by the signs that accompanied it.

Mark 16:19–20

There are times when we want to face our difficulties; but there are times when we want to leave them, and, attaining a very complete detachment, try to hear our Lord's voice saying, 'Come unto Me.'

During the time of His three years' ministry how often He said to His Apostles, 'Come unto Me,' 'Come ye apart into a desert place,' 'Come and see.' As He drew near the ship, walking on stormy waters, He said to St Peter, 'Come.' That blessed word, 'Come,' floats through the pages of the Gospel and through the ages of the years with an unspeakable tender cadence, calling tired and weary hearts and troubled minds to the one rest, the Sacred Heart of Jesus. Love calls to love, and love comes to Love.

But He says, 'Come,' in order that He may say, 'Go.' 'Go ye into all the world and teach the Gospel unto every creature, baptizing them into the Name of the Father and of the Son and of the Holy Ghost.' It is only in proportion as we come that we can, with any real service, go. When they had really come to Him, when they had learnt to feed upon Him, when they had attained to communion with Him, then He could say, 'Go out into all the world and teach, and baptize into the threefold Name.' In proportion as we really come to Him, in that proportion shall we go forth with fruitfulness. Our whole life must be made up of coming and going, coming to Jesus and going from Jesus, and yet we never leave Him, for whither He sends us He goes with us. 'Lo, I am with you always, even unto the end of the world.'

From *Meditations for Every Day*, Father Andrew SDC

*L*ord,
in our joys and in our sorrows
you invite us to come to you:
to abide in your love,
to be your disciples –
sometimes frail
fragile
fearful
hesitant,
but still you call us,
and you call us
to be sent
to be spent
to serve
and to bring hope,
to go out into the world,
to be instruments of your love.
And this we cannot do without your help.
So we remember your promise:
'I am with you always'
and rejoice in your presence.

MONDAY

Coming home

*H*ow dear to me is your dwelling, O Lord of hosts!
     My soul has a desire and longing
  for the courts of the Lord;
  my heart and my flesh rejoice in the living God.

The sparrow has found her a house
and the swallow a nest where she may lay her young,
by the side of your altars, O Lord of hosts,
my King and my God.

Happy are they who dwell in your house!
They will always be praising you.

Happy are the people whose strength is in you!
Whose hearts are set on the pilgrims' way . . .

For one day in your courts
is better than a thousand in my own room,
and to stand at the threshold of the house of my God
than to dwell in the courts of the wicked . . .

O Lord of hosts,
happy are they who put their trust in you.

Psalm 84 (selected verses), *The Revised Psalter*

In a book called *The Longing for Home* the American writer Frederick Buechner tells of his search for 'the home I long for every day of my life', and

> I believe that in my heart I have found, and have maybe always known, the way that leads to it. I believe that the home we long for and belong to is finally where Christ is. I believe that home is Christ's kingdom, which exists both within us and among us as we wend our prodigal ways through the world in search of it.

If, as Paul claims, our true homeland is in heaven, how are we to speak of that which is literally unimaginable other than in some such quickly tedious practice as that of 'casting down our golden crowns about the glassy sea'? My mind tells me that I can't do so; my heart tells me something different. That somehow the meaning of heaven is linked to the two most important lessons we have to learn on earth: how to trust and how to love. Learning to trust that the hunger I sometimes feel is not anything money can buy, but the bringing to fruition of that potential for love, those stirrings of compassion, that longing for justice, that response to beauty, those intimations of joy, that have prompted me all my life in my search for God, and drawn me inevitably, as iron filings are drawn to magnetic north, in the direction of home. And that one day that hunger will be satisfied. In her remarkable novel about the Holocaust, *Fugitive Pieces,* Anne Michaels writes:

> In experiments to determine the mechanisms of migration, scientists locked warblers in cages and kept them in

darkened rooms where they couldn't see the sky. The birds lived in bewildered twilight. Yet each October, they huddled, agitated, turned inside out with yearning. The magnetic pole pulled their blood, the thumbprint of the night sky on their inner eye.

To hope for heaven (or the Kingdom or the City of God, call it what we will) is simply to set our hunger in the context of eternity.

From *Pray, Love, Remember*, Michael Mayne

O sweet and blessed country,
  the home of God's elect!
O sweet and blessed country
that eager hearts expect!
Jesu, in mercy bring us
to that dear land of rest;
who art, with God the Father
and Spirit, ever blest.

Hymn: 'Jerusalem the Golden'

TUESDAY

The promise of the Spirit

'*All this I have spoken while still with you. But the Advocate, the Holy Spirit, whom the Father will send in my name, will teach you all things and will remind you of everything I have said to you. Peace I leave with you; my peace I give you. I do not give to you as the world gives. Do not let your hearts be troubled and do not be afraid.*

'*You heard me say, "I am going away and I am coming back to you." If you loved me, you would be glad that I am going to the Father, for the Father is greater than I. I have told you now before it happens, so that when it does happen you will believe. I will not say much more to you, for the prince of this world is coming. He has no hold over me, but he comes so that the world may learn that I love the Father and do exactly what my Father has commanded me.*

'*Come now; let us leave.*'

John 14:25–31

They've been eating supper together. Jesus gets up from the table, takes a basin of water and a towel, and proceeds to wash the feet of his disciples. Peter objects, but Jesus overrides him and continues the washing (John 13:1–11). And then Jesus begins to talk; he takes a long time – this is the longest conversation or discourse of Jesus that we have reported to us. The disciples listen. Eight times the disciples (five are named) make comments or ask questions; one-liners that Jesus weaves into the conversation (John 13:12–16:33). Finally, Jesus prays. As he prays he gathers up the life that they have lived together and fuses it into the life that the disciples will continue to live, praying his life and work and their life and work into an identity: it is going to be the same life whether people saw and heard Jesus living it or will see and hear Peter and Thomas and Philip living it (John 17).

And that's it. This is how Jesus chooses to spend that evening with his disciples preparing for the transition from Jesus present to Jesus absent. He begins by washing the feet of his disciples, down on his knees before each of them, getting his hands dirty with the dirt of their feet. He ends by praying to his Father and their Father that what they continue to do will be congruent with what he has been doing.

The pattern holds: whatever we do in Jesus' name, we begin on our knees before our friends and neighbours and conclude looking 'up to heaven' praying to the Father. Washing dirty feet and praying to the Holy Father bookend our lives. We can't live Jesus' life, we can't do Jesus' work, without doing it within the boundaries that Jesus has set.

But there is more here, much more. Between the washing and the prayer there is the conversation. Condensed into a single Jesus sentence the conversation is, 'I tell you the truth: it is to your advantage that I go away, for if I do not go away, the Advocate will not come to you; but if I go, I will send him to you' (John 16:7).

From *Christ Plays in Ten Thousand Places*, Eugene Petersen

L ord, you call us
    to abide in your love,
to be your disciples:
we come to you now —
our hearts are cold;
Lord, warm them by your selfless love.
Our hearts are sinful;
cleanse them with your precious blood.
Our hearts are weak;
strengthen them with your joyous Spirit.
Our hearts are empty;
fill them with your presence.

Lord, our hearts are yours;
possess them always
and only for
YOURSELF.

WEDNESDAY

Knowing Christ risen and ascended

*T*herefore, since we have been justified through faith, we have peace with God through our Lord Jesus Christ, through whom we have gained access by faith into this grace in which we now stand. And we boast in the hope of the glory of God. Not only so, but we also glory in our sufferings, because we know that suffering produces perseverance; perseverance, character; and character, hope. And hope does not put us to shame, because God's love has been poured out into our hearts through the Holy Spirit, who has been given to us.

Romans 5:1–5

The resurrection of Christ offers us the most powerful reminder and reassurance that we may trust God, even when everything around us is collapsing and we are unable to discern God's presence anywhere.

To know Christ is to know the total reliability of a loving and caring God, even when everything in our experience seems to point in the opposite direction. We see so much in the world that perplexes us and causes us to doubt. How can there be a God when there is so much suffering in the world? How can the resurrection be a victory over sin and death, when sin continues to be a living presence in the life of the believer and death remains the grim finality which confronts us? It is very easy for us to identify with those perplexed and agonized disciples, as the dead body of their Lord was taken down from the cross and taken away for burial. We need to hold fast to the promises of God to be with us, even when we walk in the valley of the shadow of death. There will be times when we cannot sense his presence, and when everything around us seems to proclaim his absence.

It is at those moments that the full meaning of the resurrection of Christ is to be grasped. To know Christ as the one who has been crucified and has risen is to find comfort in the knowledge of the presence of God in moments of despair and anguish – moments when we feel profoundly alone, abandoned and without any helper ...

Christianity is a religion of hope, which focuses on the resurrection and ascension of Christ as the grounds for believing and trusting in a God who is able to triumph over death, and finally gathers believers together in the New Jerusalem. Something which happened in the past – Christ's death and resurrection – has thus inaugurated something new, which will reach its final consummation in the future.

From *Knowing Christ*, Alister McGrath

B *lessed be the risen and ascended Lord;*
he has broken from the tomb
and opened for us the gate to life eternal.
Blessed be the risen and ascended Lord;
he comes to his disciples.
Where two or three are gathered together
he is there.
In fellowship, the breaking of bread and sharing his Word
he meets us.
Blessed be the risen and ascended Lord:
he comes from the dead with life,
bringing us light, joy and hope.
He crosses the boundary between earth and heaven.
Blessed be the risen and ascended Lord. Alleluia! Alleluia!

THURSDAY

The King of love

In my vision at night I looked, and there before me was one like a son of man, coming with the clouds of heaven. He approached the Ancient of Days and was led into his presence. He was given authority, glory and sovereign power; all nations and peoples of every language worshipped him. His dominion is an everlasting dominion that will not pass away, and his kingdom is one that will never be destroyed.

Daniel 7:13–14

Behind all the beautiful but inadequate words and phrases of the Ascension Collects and hymns, there stands the great spiritual truth of the kingship of Christ, the fact of Christ the King of Love. The idea of divine kingship is no new one. 'God is my king of old,' wrote the Psalmist, 'God reigneth over the nations;' 'Lift up your heads O ye gates, and be ye lifted up ye everlasting doors and the king of glory shall come in;' 'God sitteth above the water floods; the Lord remaineth a king for ever.' Such language is familiar to all religious people, but it is often misinterpreted and God is looked upon as if he were some oriental sultan needing to be placated, appeased and feared. We miss the point: 'Pilate saith unto him "Art thou the King of the Jews?" Jesus answered "My kingdom is not of this world, else would my servants fight".' It is just because of this that Christ the King dares ask as his right what no earthly king can ever hope to have – possession of ourselves of the heart and centre of our being. Other kings may demand our strength, our skill, our money, the service of our bodies or minds, but he alone it is who demands as of right you and me, ourselves, our souls and bodies, as his due. And why is it his due? Because his is a kingship not of power but of love, not of strength, but of sacrifice, a kingship in which the king demands because he gives – what? *His* whole self to our whole selves.

How does he do this? With the terrible force of love – sweeping on and on till it possesses the whole of us, for divine love can be content with nothing less. Do not suppose that divine love can be satisfied with a part; do not imagine that you can bring the Christ to your home but keep him only in the best room, specially prepared for him, leaving the other rooms with their dust and their dirt, and the skeletons in their cupboards. Bring him in at all, and he must come everywhere, and be admitted into our utmost secrets, share our inmost longings and be privy to our most hidden sins. Bring him into a part of your life and refuse to bring him further and you can know no happiness. Better indeed never to have known Christ at all than to have known him and his love, and to have kept back part of the price, to have refused the demands of his love, to have closed a door in his face on which he knocked for entry.

From *Feeding the Flock*, Glyn Simon

Father,
I abandon myself into your hands,
do with me what you will.
Whatever you may do,
I thank you.
I am ready for all,
I accept all.
Let only your will be done in me
and all your creatures –
I wish no more than this, O Lord.

Into your hands I commend my soul;
I offer it to you
with the love of my heart,
for I love you, Lord,
and need to give you myself,
to surrender myself
into your hands without reserve,
and with boundless confidence,
for you are my Father.

Charles de Foucauld

FRIDAY

Praying in the Spirit

*I*n the same way, the Spirit helps us in our weakness. We do not know what we ought to pray for, but the Spirit himself intercedes for us through wordless groans. And he who searches our hearts knows the mind of the Spirit, because the Spirit intercedes for God's people in accordance with the will of God.

Romans 8:26–7

And pray in the Spirit on all occasions with all kinds of prayers and requests. With this in mind, be alert and always keep on praying for all the Lord's people. Pray also for me, that whenever I speak, words may be given me so that I will fearlessly make known the mystery of the gospel, for which I am an ambassador in chains. Pray that I may declare it fearlessly, as I should.

Ephesians 6:18–20

The prayer of the first Christians was simply a reflection of the living Christ in their midst. It was prayer 'in his name'; and by this we mean not that a formula was added at the end of every petition, but that in all their prayer they joined themselves to the prayer of Christ himself, and knew that it was his spirit which prayed in them. The best worship they could offer was simply his self-oblation in them. Praying in that Spirit, the Christian's prayer is immersed in the ocean of the Son's communion with the Father: 'In Holy Spirit praying, keep yourselves in the love of God' (Jude 21). 'Keep your watch with continuous prayer and supplication, praying the whole time in the Spirit: with constant wakefulness and perseverance you will find opportunity to pray for all the Christian brethren' (Eph. 18, Wand translation). 'We do not even know how we ought to pray, but through our inarticulate groans the Spirit himself is pleading in us, and God who searches our inmost being knows what the Spirit means, because he pleads for God's own people in God's own way' (Rom. 8.26).

To live in prayer, therefore, is to live in the Spirit; and to live in the Spirit is to live in Christ. I am not saying that prayer is a means or a method which we have to use in order to have more of Christ in us or in order to be more fully possessed by the Spirit. I am saying something simpler and more fundamental: to live in Christ is to live in prayer. Prayer is not something you do; it is a style of living. It is living under the witness which the Spirit bears with our spirit that we are sons of God. Such a witness lays upon us the awful freedom of adult sonship. Prayer is our response to both the privilege and the responsibility whereby we cry *Abba*, Father.

Every form of prayer that is stirred by the Spirit is in essence a repetition of the love-word *Abba!*, the Jesus word. It should be to the Christian what the syllable OM is to the Hindu, to be uttered not as the exclusive talisman of one religion, but as the password of humanity, establishing in Christ the ultimate truth of everyman. Each time of prayer is an attempt to open ourselves more fully to that direct communion with the Father which Jesus knew, and to realize more deeply our relationship to him as adult sons and daughters. That communion is the primary gift of the Go-Between God and he alone can make it happen.

From *The Go-Between God*, John V. Taylor

L ord, I search for the words to address you.
  I seek for the right attitude to approach you.
Abba, Father,
help me to realise
that all I need
is to dwell in you,
letting your Spirit fill me,
making my prayer your prayer,
the Jesus prayer.

SATURDAY (EVE OF PENTECOST)

The God who surprises

' You are witnesses of these things. I am going to send you what my Father has promised; but stay in the city until you have been clothed with power from on high.'

When he had led them out to the vicinity of Bethany, he lifted up his hands and blessed them. While he was blessing them, he left them and was taken up into heaven. Then they worshipped him and returned to Jerusalem with great joy. And they stayed continually at the temple, praising God.

Luke 24:48–53

A fundamental element of Pentecost is astonishment. We know our God is a God of astonishment. No one expected anything further from the disciples after Jesus' death; they were a small, insignificant group of defeated orphans, lost without their Master. Instead, an unexpected event took place that astounded people: they were astonished to hear each of the disciples speaking in their own tongues and all talking about the marvels of God (cf. Acts 2:6–7, 11). The Church born at Pentecost is an astonishing community because a new message is proclaimed with God-given strength – the resurrection of Christ – and in a new language, the universal language of love. The disciples are adorned with power from on high and speak with courage; a few minutes earlier they huddled meekly, but now they speak with courage and candour, with the freedom of the Holy Spirit.

This is how the Church is meant to be; capable of astounding while proclaiming to all that Jesus Christ has conquered death, that God's arms are always open, that His patience is always there, waiting for us in order to heal and forgive us. Jesus arose and bestowed His Spirit on the Church for this very mission.

Remember: if the Church is alive, she must always surprise. The living Church must astound us. A Church that cannot surprise is weak, sick and dying, and needs to be taken to the emergency department as quickly as possible!

From *A Gift of Joy and Hope*, Pope Francis

*M*ay the God of surprises astonish you with the abundance
of his love.

May you receive from him that blessing which is his gift to you.

May you find in him the Way to the Lord Jesus, the Truth and
the Life.

May you, like the disciples at Pentecost, emerge from fear and
darkness

to be courageous bearers of that Light which never dims.

Lord, we pray that we may make space to listen to the still,
small voice

which challenges us to tell the world that you, our Risen Lord,

always welcome us home.

PENTECOST

FEAST OF PENTECOST

The breakthrough

*W*hen *the day of Pentecost came, they were all together in one place. Suddenly a sound like the blowing of a violent wind came from heaven and filled the whole house where they were sitting. They saw what seemed to be tongues of fire that separated and came to rest on each of them. All of them were filled with the Holy Spirit and began to speak in other tongues as the Spirit enabled them.*

Now there were staying in Jerusalem God-fearing Jews from every nation under heaven. When they heard this sound, a crowd came together in bewilderment, because each one heard their own language being spoken. Utterly amazed, they asked: 'Aren't all these who are speaking Galileans? Then how is it that each of us hears them in our native language? Parthians, Medes and Elamites; residents of Mesopotamia, Judea and Cappadocia, Pontus and Asia, Phrygia and Pamphylia, Egypt and the parts of Libya near Cyrene; visitors from Rome (both Jews and converts to Judaism); Cretans and Arabs – we hear them declaring the wonders of God in our own tongues!' Amazed and perplexed, they asked one another, 'What does this mean?'

Some, however, made fun of them and said, 'They have had too much wine.'

Acts 2:1–13

When Moses went up Mount Sinai the people were warned twice not to come near (Exodus 19:12, 21). God's presence was too dangerous for them and could only be encountered by Moses, or Moses and Aaron. The revelation of God in the Old Testament was kept for only a few, special people like Moses, Elijah and Isaiah. All others were kept away lest the revelation prove too much for them. In Acts 2 no one is kept away. The Holy Spirit does not just descend on Peter, or on Peter, James and John, but upon all the people who were gathered there, and then, subsequently, on all those who heard and responded to the message. One of the wonderful things about our Christian faith is that nothing is secret or exclusive. Everything is open to everyone. This is a vital strand that runs through the New Testament, beginning with the ministry of Jesus, re-enforced here at Pentecost, and again and again in the writings of Paul.

It may be reinforced but somehow we still struggle to come to terms with it. Christian gatherings of all sorts fall too easily into exclusivity: where some belong and others do not; where some feel themselves at the centre and others about as unwelcome as they can be. This is one of those places where living Spirit-filled lives is at odds with human instinct. The Holy Spirit continues to pour into our lives, refusing to observe boundaries that pronounce on those who are worthy and those who are not, those who are 'in' and those who are 'out'. The coming of the Holy Spirit at Pentecost flings wide the doors, declaring that all are welcome, that no one is to keep away. We are no longer told, as the Israelites were, 'not to break through to the Lord' (Exodus 19:21) because the Lord breaks through to us over and over again, if only we will let him.

From *This Risen Existence*, Paula Gooder

*C*ome, Holy Spirit.
   Come like the dew to refresh us.
Come like fire to consume us.
Come like the wind to disturb us.
Come, stir our minds to search for the Truth.
Come with joy to disperse our sorrows.
Come with your mighty power to enthuse us.
Come now, Holy Spirit, break through to us
and help us to open the doors that are shut.
Come, break down the barriers that divide us.
Come to expand our horizons.
Come to transform us and all your people
that we may live and work to your glory.
For you are our generous God, who has shown
your love for us in Jesus the Lord,
risen, ascended, glorified. Amen.

The Writers

David Adam – until his retirement was Vicar of Holy Island where his work involved ministering to thousands of pilgrims and visitors. He has published several books of prayers composed in the Celtic pattern.

Father Andrew SDC – an Anglican priest who worked in the East End of London where he founded the Society of Divine Compassion, the first of the Anglican religious orders for men. He was highly regarded as a spiritual guide and was also a poet, artist and writer.

Patrick Appleford – an English Anglican priest and hymn-writer. He founded the Twentieth Century Church Light Music Group.

Mark Barrett – Abbot in the Benedictine community of Worth Abbey.

Anthony Bloom – consecrated bishop in 1958 and Archbishop in 1962, in 1966 he was raised to the rank of Metropolitan in the Russian Orthodox Church. He built up a considerable reputation as a spiritual writer and authority on the spiritual life.

Sister Maria Boulding – was a contemplative nun, a member of the Benedictine community formerly at Stanbrook Abbey but now relocated to North Yorkshire. Her books include *Marked for Life, The Coming of God* and *Gateway to Hope.*

Carlo Carretto – one of the Little Brothers of Jesus, an order inspired by Charles de Foucauld, he spent his last years, after living the eremitical life in the Sahara, as a hermit in Umbria. Among his books are *The God Who Comes, Letters from the Desert, In Search of Beyond* and *Love is for Living.*

Rex Chapman – was an Anglican chaplain in Aberdeen University with a gift for relating the situations in which we find ourselves today to the world that Jesus knew and the faith he taught.

Stephen Cherry – formerly Director of Ministerial Training for Durham diocese and a Residentiary Canon of Durham Cathedral, he is currently Dean of King's College, Cambridge.

Stephen Cottrell – the Archbishop of York, previously Bishop of Chelmsford and before that Bishop of Reading. He has written widely on evangelism, spirituality and discipleship. Among his books are *On Priesthood* (2020), a series of Lent and Holy Week meditations, and more recently *Dear England* and *Godforsaken.*

Maggi Dawn – an Anglican priest, currently chaplain and Fellow of Robinson College, Cambridge, where she teaches theology. She is the author of several hymns and worship songs.

Austin Farrer – an Anglican priest, theologian and biblical scholar, he was Warden of Keble College, Oxford, and a prolific writer. His books include several on St Mark and numerous collections of sermons.

Charles de Foucauld – was French Catholic priest. He lived as a hermit among the Tuareg people in the Sahara in Algeria.

Pope Francis – the first Pope of the Americas, Jorge Mario Bergoglio, hails from Argentina. He was elected Supreme Pontiff on 13 March 2013.

Luigi Gioia – a freelance writer who also lectures in theology and spirituality. He leads retreats, workshops and study days in the UK, the USA and many other countries while based as Assistant Priest at St Paul's, Knightsbridge, in London.

Paula Gooder – a freelance writer and lecturer in biblical studies. She is also a Chancellor at St Paul's Cathedral and Canon Theologian of Birmingham Cathedral. A well-known writer, she is also in great demand as a lecturer.

Margaret Guenther – a priest, writer, spiritual director and grandmother. Since her first publication, *Holy Listening*, she has written a number of books on the spiritual life.

John Hadley – an Anglican priest who served as a university chaplain, chaplain to an ecumenical community and a parish priest. He is the author of *Bread for the World: Christ and the Eucharist Today*.

Edwin Hatch – was an English theologian and joined the Church of England in 1853 and took Holy Orders. He was a professor of classics in Trinity College, Toronto, from 1859 to 1862, when he became rector of the high school at Quebec. In 1867 he returned to Oxford, and was made Vice-Principal of St Mary Hall, a post which he held until 1885.

Gerard W. Hughes – a spiritual writer and Jesuit priest. Hughes published a number of books; his most well-known book is *God of Surprises* (1985).

Trystan Owain Hughes – theologian and historian, he was Anglican chaplain for Cardiff University and Vicar of Christ Church, Cardiff, before his appointment as Director of Ministry for the Church in Wales.

Cardinal Basil Hume – from the age of eighteen he was a member of the Benedictine monastery at Ampleforth where he was abbot from 1963 to 1976 when he became Archbishop of Westminster.

Brother Jonathan – of the Benedictine community of Worth Abbey.

Clive Staples Lewis – an English writer and lay theologian. He held academic posts in English literature at Oxford and Cambridge. In addition to his scholarly work he wrote several popular novels including the Narnia fantasies for children.

Robert Llewelyn – was for fourteen years chaplain of the Shrine of Mother Julian of Norwich. He was awarded the UK individual Templeton Prize in 1994 and the Cross of St Augustine in 1998, both in recognition of his contribution to literature in Christian spirituality.

Alister McGrath – Professor of Historical Theology and former Principal of Wycliffe Hall, Oxford. One of the most important Christian authors of our times, he has written many books including *The Journey*, *To Know and Serve God*, *Why Does God Allow Suffering?* and *The NIV Bible Commentary*.

Brian D. McLaren – an evangelical pastor, author, speaker, activist and networker among innovative Christian leaders. He is the writer of many books including *A New Kind of Christianity*, *A Generous Orthodoxy* and *Naked Spirituality*. He lives in Florida and has an itinerant ministry.

Sister Margaret Magdalen – is an Anglican nun and a member of the Community of St Mary the Virgin, based at Wantage. Her previous works include *Transformed by Love: The Way of St Mary Magdalen* and *Jesus, Man of Prayer*.

Michael Mayne – was Dean of Westminster having served in parishes in south London and Hertfordshire and as Vicar of Great St Mary's Cambridge, the University Church. Previously he was Head of Religious Broadcasting at the BBC. Among his publications are *A Year Lost and Found* and *The Sunrise of Wonder*.

Eric Milner-White – was a British Anglican priest, academic and decorated military chaplain. He was a founder of the Oratory of the Good Shepherd, an Anglican dispersed community. From 1941 to 1963, he was the Dean of York in the Church of England.

Henri Nouwen – a Dutch Catholic priest. He spent twenty years teaching in the Netherlands and the United States and gave his final years to teaching and ministering at L'Arche Daybreak Community in Toronto. A prolific writer, his books include *The Wounded Healer*, *The Return of the Prodigal Son*, *Here and Now* and *The Way of the Heart*.

Eugene Petersen – a pastor, theologian, writer and poet, he is the author of the contemporary paraphrase of the Bible *The*

Message, as well as *Eat This Book*, *The Jesus Way* and *Christ Plays in Ten Thousand Places*.

Timothy Radcliffe – a Dominican friar, who taught theology at Oxford and was involved in ministering to people with AIDS. He is the author of *Sing a New Song*, *I Call You Friends*, *Why Go to Church?*, *What is the Point of Being a Christian?* and *Take the Plunge*.

Brother Ramon – was an Anglican Franciscan who lived the hermit life at the monastery at Glasshampton. He wrote many books including *The Heart of Prayer*, *Franciscan Spirituality*, *The Flame of Sacred Love* and *The Prayer Mountain*.

Richard Rohr – is an American Roman Catholic Franciscan priest, a writer and speaker on spirituality. He is the founder of the Centre for Action and Contemplation and is a well-known writer and contributor to a series of daily online meditations.

Annabel Shilson-Thomas – is an Anglican priest in Cambridge. She was previously a staff writer for the development agency CAFOD.

Glyn Simon – after a curacy in Crewe he became successively warden of the Church Hostel, Bangor, and St Michael's College, Llandaff. He was Dean of Llandaff prior to becoming Bishop of Swansea and Brecon. Translated to Llandaff he became Archbishop of Wales.

Tom Smail – after ministry in the Baptist tradition in Scotland and Northern Ireland he joined the Fountain Trust promoting charismatic renewal. Ordained in the Anglican

Church he then became Vice-Principal at St John's College, Nottingham, prior to retirement in 1994.

John V. Taylor – described as priest, poet and prophet he was at one time General Secretary of the Church Missionary Society which enabled him to travel widely and to visit Christian communities all over the world. He ended his days as Bishop of Winchester. As a talented writer his *The Go-Between God* won for him the Collins Religious Book Award in 1973.

William Temple – he served as Bishop of Manchester, Archbishop of York and Archbishop of Canterbury. He wrote constantly and produced a popular devotional commentary on St John's Gospel, *Readings from St John's Gospel*. He was a political and social reformer and a popular leader in the Anglican Church.

Desmond Tutu – ordained as an Anglican priest he was appointed the first black Dean of Johannesburg. He was Bishop of Lesotho, Secretary General of the South African Council of Churches and Archbishop of Capetown before his retirement. He was the author of several collections of sermons and numerous books.

Stephen Verney – was Canon at St George's Chapel, Windsor, and subsequently on the staff of Coventry Cathedral before becoming Bishop of Repton. Throughout his ministry he was much involved in training clergy and lay people in mission and spirituality.

Andrew Walker – Vicar of St Michael-in-Lewes and a Visiting Scholar at Sarum College, Salisbury. He is also Director of the London-based Ignatian Spirituality course.

J. Neville Ward – was an English Methodist minister who served in an ecumenical parish in Canterbury and as a chaplain to London University. Among his well-known books are *A Kind of Praying, Friday Afternoon* and *Five for Sorrow, Ten for Joy* (a consideration of the Rosary).

Rowan Williams – a distinguished theologian, writer and poet and former Archbishop of Canterbury. Much of his early life was spent in academia before becoming Bishop of Monmouth and Archbishop of Wales then the 104th Archbishop of Canterbury. Prior to retirement he was Master of Magdalen College, Cambridge. He has written extensively.

Tom Wright – was Bishop of Durham but after some years returned to university life to become Research Professor of New Testament and Early Christianity at the University of St Andrews. He is a prolific writer on theological subjects sometimes under the name N. T. Wright.

Text Credits

Page 67: Copyright © Sydney Carter (1915–2004) Lord of the Dance: verse 5 and chorus © 1963 Stainer & Bell Ltd.

Page 70: Copyright © Timothy Radcliffe, *Why Go to Church?*, 2008, Continuum Publishing, an imprint of Bloomsbury Publishing Plc.

Page 74: Copyright © Anthony Bloom, *Meditations on a Theme*, 2003, Continuum Publishing, an imprint of Bloomsbury Publishing Plc.

Page 90: Copyright © Rex Chapman. Poem and prayer from *A Kind of Praying*, 1970. Published by SCM Press. Used by permission. rights@hymnsam.co.uk

Page 102: Copyright © Luigi Gioia, *Say it to God*, 2017, Continuum Publishing, an imprint of Bloomsbury Publishing Plc.

Page 106: Copyright © Luigi Gioia, *Say it to God*, 2017, Continuum Publishing, an imprint of Bloomsbury Publishing Plc.

Page 128: Copyright © Timothy Radcliffe, *What is the Point of Being a Christian?*, 2005, Continuum Publishing, an imprint of Bloomsbury Publishing Plc.

Page 164: Words from *Lord Jesus Christ* © 1960 Josef Weinbeger Limited. Reproduced by permission of the copyright owners.

Page 174: Copyright © C. S. Lewis, *Miracles*, 1947, 1960 C. S. Lewis Pte. Ltd. Extract reprinted by permission.

Thanks

I am most grateful to Andrew Lyon, Jessica Lacey and the team at Hodder & Stoughton for all their help in getting this anthology published; to Kathleen Boyce for editing the prayers; and to my wife Margaret for her continued support and encouragement.

About the Compiler

Arthur Howells is a retired Anglican priest who has served the whole of his ministry in the Church in Wales. He is married to Margaret, a retired schoolteacher. Formerly Canon Residentiary and Chancellor of Brecon Cathedral, he was Canon Missioner of the Diocese of Swansea and Brecon for ten years prior to his last appointment as Vicar of St James', Swansea. He has compiled four anthologies – *A Lent Companion, Generous Love, The Little Book of Lent* and *The Little Book of Advent* – and is the author of *A Franciscan Way of Life: Brother Ramon's Quest for Holiness.*